Social Theory in Education
PRIMER

PETER LANG
New York • Washington, D.C./Baltimore • Bern
Frankfurt am Main • Berlin • Brussels • Vienna • Oxford

Philip Wexler

Social Theory in Education PRIMER

PETER LANG
New York • Washington, D.C./Baltimore • Bern
Frankfurt am Main • Berlin • Brussels • Vienna • Oxford

Library of Congress Cataloging-in-Publication Data

Wexler, Philip.
Social theory in education primer / Philip Wexler.
p. cm.
Includes bibliographical references and index.
1. Educational sociology. 2. Social sciences—Philosophy.
3. Durkheim, Émile, 1858-1917. 4. Marx, Karl, 1813-1883.
5. Weber, Max, 1864–1920. I. Title.
LC189.W48   306.43—dc22   2008042027
ISBN 978-1-4331-0337-7

Bibliographic information published by **Die Deutsche Bibliothek**.
Die Deutsche Bibliothek lists this publication in the "Deutsche
Nationalbibliografie"; detailed bibliographic data is available
on the Internet at http://dnb.ddb.de/.

Cover design by Clear Point Designs

The paper in this book meets the guidelines for permanence and durability
of the Committee on Production Guidelines for Book Longevity
of the Council of Library Resources.

Printed in the United States of America

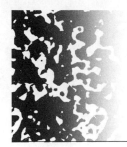

Contents

CHAPTER ONE

Introduction: Three Models of Social Theory in Education

Why do we need a book on social theory in education? First, because Education as a practical activity and as a field of academic study is dominated by Psychology. The isolated individual is studied, and individual traits are measured and compared. Second, because more social approaches are generally either narrowly focused on very specific empirical researches, or they talk in broad political terms about what Education ought to be like and how it can change society.

What is missing in all these approaches is a systematic understanding of how to understand education as a social process. Why this more systematic or theoretical social approach is missing or underrepresented in Education is itself a social question. A contextual or reflexive view of knowledge, including fields of study and practice such as Education, puts all knowledge in its **context** and tries to understand how the dynamics of the social and cultural shape the content, form, and direction of knowledge.

Context

A shorthand way of talking about the array and constellation of social factors and forces in any situation. In our discussion, context influences knowledge, and being aware of that is referred to as reflexivity.

Social Theory

When we talk about social theory, we mean a coherent understanding of social processes. This understanding uses

concepts and relies on careful observation and experience, in order to try to achieve generalizations. Even in defining what is social theory, however, there are different views among social analysts. On the one hand, are the sociologists who work in sociology departments in universities and have a very clear idea that their research and theory are "scientific" in a way no different from any other field of knowledge recognized as science. At the other end of the spectrum, are people who try to make sense of the organization of social processes within social life, people who are not professional sociologists and may not even be affiliated with formal professional organizations such as universities. In this book, we will include the works of all types of social theorists. In contemporary work, because of our combined focus on social theory and education, we will find social theorists in Education as well as in Sociology, and some of the most important, entirely outside of the academy.

Our emphasis is on what is called the "classical tradition," meaning those social theorists who have most influenced the way we think about society, either within academic settings or in social life in general. This emphasis, I think, has been lacking in current thinking about education in society, even though many use the basic ideas of classical social theory without knowing it. In working with students interested in critical pedagogy, for example, or in globalization and education, multiculturalism, gender studies, and teacher education, it has been surprising to see how much of this tradition has seeped into people's language and understanding, without their being consciously aware of the more articulated and systematic set of concepts and researches from which their almost commonsense way of doing social theory derives. This book will provide a key: classical social theory. Using this key, we can, I think, organize almost all social theory and research in education in a clear and straightforward manner.

"Theory is a 'story' about how and why events in the universe occur," writes Jonathan Turner (1991; 1) in *The Structure of Sociological Theory*—one of the most influential professional sociological theory textbooks. He continues: "Sociological theory thus seeks to explain how and why humans behave, interact and organize themselves in certain ways." Turner, who is closer to our first, "scientific" side of the spectrum, goes on to specify the elements that make up formal theories in science. Sociology,

he observes, does not quite make it to the mold of a formal or paradigm scientific theory. Rather, he notes:

> Much of what is labeled as sociological theory is, in reality, only a loose clustering of implicit assumptions, some basic concepts, and various kinds of theoretical statements and formats. But none of these is dominant or sufficiently precise to constitute a paradigm…most sociological theory constitutes a verbal "image of society" rather than a rigorously constructed set of theoretical statements organized into a logically coherent format. (Turner, 1991; 29–30)

What will be developed in this book is a view of theory that is somewhere between a strictly scientific approach and a more general image-, visions-, or ideas-about-society approach. We share not only the explanatory interest of the scientific social theorists, but also the view that much understanding can be gained through the lens of general ideas and not necessarily only from tightly connected and research-based concepts about how society works. Perhaps that is why we use the word "models," rather than either "paradigms" or "visions." For in a model, the parts fit together, and it aims to show us how the world, or a specific phenomenon in the world, works. We are interested in an understanding that uses concepts in interpreting the social world, even when they are not perfectly integrated or proven. It is neither a fully specified certainty nor a vision loaded with hopes and aspirations, but rather a way of making sense of social processes.

This is probably closer to Randall Collins' (1994) understanding of social theory. He too has an interpretive, explanatory interest in making sense of social processes. While he writes about a more specifically and professionally focused discipline of sociology, he also places social understanding in its historical context. He sees social knowledge both in terms of contextual, environmental, social, institutional, and cultural influences that shape it, and as well as in terms of traditions of social understanding. Our models, based on the three most well-known founders of the main sociological traditions, go forward from there, not only to contemporary theorists, but also—more importantly and differently than almost all other work in social theory—to understand social analyses of education.

So, we begin with sociologists, in their efforts to define what theory is, to develop a theory that makes sense of social life and,

in some cases, to reflect on how these theories are shaped by the context. Given the educational interest, we do not want to get stuck in the internal debates of sociological theorists, or to become so interested in the historical context of social theory that we forget why we ever began to ask these questions. Our aim is to show how social thinking and research about education can be organized as different models of social processes applied to education. Still, our models are deeply implicated in their histories and social contexts.

What is important in the context that has shaped sociology? For Collins, the development of sociology is part of a history of the development of the social sciences, particularly in Western Europe, during the eighteenth century (Collins, 1994; 16):

> For the social sciences the takeoff period was the 1700s. In a characteristic burst of self-confidence, the thinkers of the time referred to their era as the **Enlightenment**. (bold not in the original)

The Enlightenment is a very general name for a series of social, intellectual movements of the eighteenth century, which, as we shall see, is identified particularly with the triumph of the natural scientific way of thinking and approaching the world as privileged—valued above all other ways of thinking and being. We can also think of the Enlightenment as the intellectual core of a much wider set of social habits and culture that is called "modern." For now, it is important only to note that sociology, as the disciplinary main line and base of social theory, itself has a history and is itself influenced by the social context.

The particular social understanding of the development of sociology that Collins wants to put forward is that more than the other human and social sciences—especially more than psychology—sociology, belatedly, becomes an organized and influential body of knowledge in part through finding its place in universities. Supposedly, this grants a certain distance from everyday life, which enables sociologists to seek more generalized concepts and theories. At the same time—and this is its specialness—sociology is historically more closely linked to political movements. Its incorporation or institutionalization within universities is not fully successful. In a sense, sociology was marginal, between politics and the new "moral sciences" of

Enlightenment

Indicates the leading social, intellectual movement of the eighteenth century, where the scientific path of knowledge, as developed particularly by Newton becomes the general cultural ideal. In that sense, Enlightenment can be thought of as the intellectual core of modernity. Its central commitment is to reason, understood according to the natural science model. This commitment implies also that reason—and not faith, belief, and emotion—provides the direction and means toward greater human freedom and self-realization in society.

the eighteenth century, which try to put understanding of human affairs within the grid of natural science. "Most important for the development of sociology were individuals who combined a university orientation with their political and popular interests" (Collins, 1994; 39). This tension for social theorists—between the more socially detached analytical interest of the natural science view and the socially involved politics of a variety of social movements—characterizes both the classical and the contemporary social theorists in education.

Still another approach to understanding what is social theory underlines, as we do, the centrality of classical sociology. Also, it takes the approach that both the tradition and context of social theory should be considered. Finally, as in our approach, the underlying interest here too is in showing that the continuing value of classical social theory is in making sense socially. Tradition and context are important. What is most important is whether a social theory works—whether it enhances our understanding. Once we can use the concepts of social theory, do we see everyday social life, social processes, social organization, and their historical contexts differently and more clearly?

George McCarthy's (2003) view is different than either Turner's or Collins' about the nature of social theory and its context. The history of classical sociology is better understood not by looking back a hundred and fifty or two hundred years from when Emile Durkheim, Karl Marx, and Max Weber wrote, but much further, to ancient Greece. McCarthy argues that the Enlightenment's influence on sociology is less the result of its historical, institutional origins (which is Collins' claim), and more the result of a twentieth-century American lens that favors the scientist-model of Enlightenment science. Durkheim, Marx, and Weber should not so much be interpreted and taught as the precursors of a modern "science of sociology." That is an American invention, asserts McCarthy, fostered by sociologists such as Talcott Parsons (whom we shall later encounter in our placement of him within the Durkheimian tradition).

Instead, we ought to see the formative social theorists of our times, who were all born in the nineteenth century and wrote during that time and, in some cases, into the twentieth century, influenced by the social ideas of the ancient Greek philosophers. Moreover, they were really less interested in being scientists than

in being social critics. Social theory, then, in this view, is not a positive science but a practice of social criticism rooted in ancient visions and political ideals.

McCarthy is very tough about how he sees classical social theory as being misinterpreted, especially in America (2003; 2):

> American sociologists embraced the Enlightenment with its Cartesian dualisms and scientific rationality; its method of causal determinism and explanatory laws; its political philosophy of possessive individualism and liberal rights; and its economic theory of utilitarian values, market freedoms, and consumer choices.

Opposing the view that the founding sociologists were expressing an Enlightenment view of social theory, McCarthy is persuaded that their own education in the ancient Greek philosophers created for them ideals of social justice and civic virtue. Reading Aristotle and other ancient philosophers made them into social critics more than natural scientists (McCarthy, 2003; 11):

> All were trained in classical Greek political science. Although expressed in various ways and to different degrees, by returning to the dreams of the ancients, they developed a critique of the Enlightenment and classical liberalism; held nostalgic views of the moral community and its cultural values and social goals; were critical of the reification and social pathologies of industrial society in their theories of alienation and exploitation, rationalization and the iron cage, and organic solidarity and anomie; rejected the precepts of laissez-faire economics and utilitarianism.

We can infer from the above quote that there are not only very different views about what social theory is, but also—even when we get into specific social theories, ones that we think are formative for social analyses of education in our times—differences of opinion or, more accurately, of interpretation.

I took the middle ground on what the form of social theory is, between imitation of strict natural science and general societal images or visions. As we get into the specific theories, especially the ones that I think have been foundational for social analyses of education, you will see that I take a middle ground here too. Not out of timidity, I hope, but in the belief that the most important social theorists were divided within themselves. Turner's view of sociology as potentially a sort of positive natural science, and Collins' historical institutional emphasis on the origins of sociology within the Enlightenment mold, and McCarthy's claim that although they might have been nineteenth-century Europeans, they were certainly not twentieth-century American scientists and were, in fact, influenced by the political social ideals of ancient Greece—all these views carry some credence.

I think so because we can show, of course, in varying degrees, that classical social theorists themselves expressed a certain two-sidedness to their thinking. They were often conflicted, as we can see in their writings, between the Enlightenment and a criticism not only of scientific reason, but also of the virtues—or, more to the point, the lack of virtues—of the social contexts in which they lived. They were both scientists and social critics. They had a mixed attitude toward their own social realities, and this ambivalence, which is expressed in their analyses of the "how" and "why" explanations, represents the torn, conflicted times in which they lived. In this sense, classical social theory articulates in its models of social interpretation what we might call the ambivalence of modernity.

Before we tackle these conflicts and the seeming contradictions that the founding giants of social theory struggled with, we need to remember what our major task is.

We are going to describe social theories and work to show how they make sense of education. But, we take a contextual view of these theories. Social theories of education belong to particular sociohistorical contexts and are themselves part of more general nonacademic cultures. Our view is that the social theories of education that we are going to describe belong to the historical time of modernity. The concepts and terms of these theories reflect the culture of their times. As I hinted, even the conflicts, contradictions, and ambivalencies represented in the social theories of education reflect the hopes, aspirations, fears, and social problems of a particular time in history. Social theories are about making sense of phenomena such as education, but they are also statements about historical cultures and their underlying, deep concerns.

Our interest, while we are being contextual and modest, is also to explain. Unlike imperialistic and scientifically unjustified claims often made by university disciplines that their knowledge is timeless and beyond historical contexts, we recognize and acknowledge from the beginning that our explanations of education as a social

process are part of more general historical cultures. At the same time, these theories can go beyond the particular contexts in which they originate and continue to offer insights and understanding of how the social world works in a more general way. This more modest contextual view of social theory also recognizes the value of cross-contextual traditions of knowledge. These traditions of knowledge represent continuity as well as context. They articulate what is important to make sense of or understand and how to do that. The "how" is by theorizing, by constructing concepts that seem to capture what is really going on and thus enable us to grasp phenomena intellectually to provide a systematic meaning that can be communicated and tested in practice.

There is a tradition of theorizing about society. Indeed, there are a number of traditions in social theory. In what follows, I have chosen three of what I see as the most important traditions of social theory. Each tradition represents a set of social commitments, a clear sense of what is socially problematic, as well as visions of possible futures. Significantly, for all the complexity and contradiction within each, these traditions of knowledge offer coherent sets of concepts or **models** of how to make sense of social processes. The origins of these models are in what is increasingly now called "**classical sociology**," whose founding thinkers are the giants who created models of how to make sense of a variety of social processes and of how to put them together in overall coherent social theories.

Classical sociology is not entirely, but for the most part, very much based on the social theories of Emile Durkheim, Karl Marx, and Max Weber. I am going to present my interpretation of these foundational models. Each of these different ways of understanding has implications for how to think about education socially. Not every classical sociologist was centrally or even marginally concerned with education. But, each model has profound implications for how we conceptualize education, for how we imagine the social character of education, for understanding the meaning of education as a social process. We start from models of social life and draw implications for education, even when the original classical sociologists themselves did not do so.

We are justified in drawing implications from classical sociology to education in part, I think, because these models continue to underlie contemporary theory and research in education that

Model

A very general term for sets of concepts that fit together to describe and explain phenomena. In our use, classical sociology is the source of different social models, or systems of explanation.

Classical Sociology

Ordinarily refers to the most well-known European sociologists of the late nineteenth and early twentieth century who influenced the basic concepts, theories, and questions of later sociologists, including modern American sociologists.

share a social orientation. Classical sociological theories are the origin of traditions of knowledge of how to think socially about education. If we examine research studies of education, we can see how much research in education implicitly and tacitly can be understood as falling within the orbit of one of the classical models, and of being influenced by them in what to study and in how to think about the phenomena under consideration. Not only research in education but also contemporary more general theories about society can be shown to represent and continue the traditions of knowledge that were first expressed in the models of classical sociology.

We are going to review both specific exemplary studies in Education as well as selected contemporary social theories. They can both be nested within classical models. Certainly there is change as well as continuity in social understandings of education that result from empirical research in education and new developments in general social theory. The organizing premise of this introductory book is that by focusing on the basic ideas of each model and by taking three traditions of knowledge that have their beginnings in the classical sociology of the late nineteenth and early twentieth-century great moderns, we can cast a wide net that carries us into the present.

The three models, beginning respectively, with the works of Emile Durkheim, Karl Marx, and Max Weber, all try to offer coherent, systematic conceptual portraits of how society works, of what matters in social life, of how larger, collective social processes effect and are expressed in the lives of individuals. Although they share a social focus, exactly which aspects of the social are most important and how they are actually embodied and enacted in collective history and individual biography (Mills, 1959) are different for each model. In that sense, they offer competing visions of social structure and of social dynamics, as well as of the relation between the collective and the individual or of social psychology. Important for us is that the implications of each model for the social interpretation of education are different.

The "educational faith" of this small book is that for all the complexities, contradictions, and discontinuities within and across models between classical sociological theory and contemporary social theory and in gaps between social theory and educational research, much is to be gained by organizing our social

understanding of education within the framework of classical sociology. In the end, we want to come away with a good conceptual map of social models of education. My bet is that the clearest and most honest way to do that is by acknowledging the continuing power of social theories conceived during the modern era to still contribute an ordering sensibility to us, in our struggle to create a meaningful interpretation of our own times and lives, and of the place of education within our own historical social context.

Context and Characters

Context

The interest in relating social theory to the social contexts in which it was first developed and later elaborated and applied is more than modesty. We are not just saying, "Ok, we recognize that social theory, and maybe all of social science (and, more radically, even, natural sciences) is an historical cultural creation of people and not something given, that is found in nature. So, we should be modest, tentative and recognize that it may change." Rather, the importance of the context is that it gets represented, though not in simple or automatic ways, in the content of the theories. This perspective, that ideas have a social basis, is the core insight of what is called, sensibly, the sociology of knowledge.

Karl Mannheim (1936), an early to mid-twentieth-century sociologist, generalized the well-worn observation that in politics, people often take up ideas that reflect and further their own social and economic practical interests. Moreover, they present these ideas to everyone else, and even to themselves, not as particular ideas that are specific to their special interests. Rather, they claim that they are general truths and apply to everyone. Of course, in the heat of political conflicts, opponents often recognize what they are doing and "unmask" the particular that masquerades as a general truth.

What Mannheim realized is that this link between the social bases, conditions, and contexts, on the one hand, and ideas, theories, and beliefs, on the other, is not only the case in obvious political conflicts. In fact, all ideas, especially ideas about the social world, can be shown to represent the social positions of their presenters or, as Max Weber called them, their "carriers." As we shall see, Karl Marx's theories about ideas and about social position and power are at the root of Mannheim's theory. Marx developed

a "critique of ideology," influenced by the critical ideas of the French philosophers of the early modern or the Enlightenment era who were writing a century before him.

Sociology of knowledge is a bit tricky. On the one hand, we want to know where our concepts and ideas come from—not only as inherited tradition from our analytical predecessors, but also as a result of our contextual influences and theirs. At the same time, we want to use these ideas, concepts, and theories to make sense of the world. Can we rely on them, if they are originally socially interested? The tentative answer is yes, if we use them carefully, checking out their logical consistency and coherence, and their realistic correspondence to what we are trying to make sense of.

Exploring the social bases of ideas can give us valuable insights into their perspectives and commitments, without thoroughly "debunking" them—provided, I think, that we are also empirical. Furthermore, this sociology of knowledge approach gives us clues not only about the history of the conceptual tools that we use but also about our own contexts, leading us to ask questions about how our thinking is itself influenced by our own social times.

So, what do we mean when we say that sociology is "modern"? Like the term "social theory," "modern" too has multiple meanings and even different time frames as to when the modern era is. Stephen Toulmin, a highly regarded contemporary philosopher, takes up this question. He also engages in a historical, contextual analysis. Similarly, he too is interested in the contemporary relevance of one of the "ancestors" of his own discipline for their contemporary relevance. In order to understand what he considers a significant change both in the context and in the appropriate theoretical model for philosophy, Toulmin explores the meaning of the term modernity (Toulmin, 1990; 5):

> Raise these questions and ambiguity takes over. Some people date the origin of modernity to the year 1436, with Gutenberg's adoption of moveable type; some to A.D. 1520. and Luther's rebellion against Church authority; others to 1648, and the Thirty Years' War; others to the American or French Revolution of 1776 or 1789; while modern times start for a few only in 1895, with Freud's Interpretation of Dreams and the rise of "modernism" in the fine arts and literature...the starting date for Modernity belongs where many historians already put it: somewhere in the period from 1600 to 1650.

Toulmin has his own particular theoretical interest. He wants to show, as he puts it, that in philosophy, modernity is "over and done with." He argues for a philosophy that goes back to a time before the modern era and the philosophers of the Enlightenment, to a previous century and the ideas of the Renaissance. Part of his argument has to do with "context" itself. Toulmin's own critique of his field is that academic philosophers have too long preferred abstract and de-contextualized forms of thought, as against more contextualized ways of thinking. He criticizes the early modern thinkers: "they disclaimed any serious interest in four differ-ent kinds of practical knowledge: the oral, the particular, the local, and the timely (1990; 30)." In other words, philosophy had become too general, in a way conforming too much to the natural science model that has become the preferred example of what is the best way to understand the world.

This natural science model is the ideal of the central philo-sophical movement of the modern era, the Enlightenment. Broadly speaking, its keynote is reason and science. It is an intellectual social movement that sees in its own commitment to modeling all knowledge as a strict version of natural science as progress over the religious orientation (and over its emphasis on faith, intuition, and emotion) and as systematic (but not empirical knowledge). This scientific rationalism of the Enlightenment is the intellectual hallmark of modernity. Toulmin, almost sociologist-like, finds part of the reason for the success of this intellectual movement in the social context in which it developed. Rationalism provides, he argues, a worldview of stability and hierarchy that compensates for the cultural and social disarray of the preceding era of religious wars. In a sense, it is a compensatory reaction that continued to triumph, long after the social conditions of its origin had changed. In Mannheim's terms, that is precisely how he defines what an ideology is—an empirically unjustified political belief.

Toulmin (1990; 104) critically characterizes this social, intellectual movement that begins in the late seventeenth century and continues into the eighteen century as "rationalism":

> The three dreams of the Rationalists thus turn out to be aspects
> of a larger dream. The dreams of a rational method, a unified
> science, and an exact language, united in a single project. All of
> them are designed to "purify" the operations of human reason by

de-contextualizing them; i.e., by divorcing them from the details of particular historical and cultural situations.

He concludes (1990; 105): "Instead, we must try to recapture the practical modesty of the humanists, which let them live free of anxiety, despite uncertainty, ambiguity, and pluralism." Frankly, I am glad that we are not the only ones counseling theoretical modesty, hearing the same advice for contemporary philosophers as for we social theorists of education.

With all due respect to Toulmin, intellectual traditions do not just go away, sometimes not even after the social situation in which they first flourished has itself been deeply altered. The foundational figures of social theory, Durkheim, Marx, and Weber, were all deeply influenced by the philosophy of the Enlightenment, a century after its triumphal time. In the later modernity of the "sociologists" (Marx was formally neither a sociologist nor a university academic), there is already an ambivalence toward the rationalist ideals of the earlier modernity of Enlightenment. Sometimes, it is a very evident, gut-wrenching ambivalence, as it was for Weber in his theory—and in his life. At other times, the tensions and contradictions within the theories surface unintentionally. Nevertheless, the sociological heritage is, in the main, influenced by its origins in modern Enlightenment theory. McCarthy (2003), whose ideas about what is classical social theory we discussed before, wants to give a loud voice to this critical anti-rationalist side of the great sociologists. After we review the three models of social theory in education, you will be in a better position to begin to formulate your own view.

For now, we want to acknowledge the power of this historical, cultural, and intellectual movement for setting the tone of sociological theory and method. This tone is a secular, even antireligious one. It sets out an empirical, analytical sort of scientific knowledge as the way of thinking and being in the world. Peter Gay, in his multivolume work on the history of the Enlightenment, puts it this way (1969; 17):

> The advance of knowledge, whether devout Christians liked it or not, meant the advance of reason. In the course of the eighteenth century, the world, at least the world of the literature, was being emptied of mystery. Pseudo science was giving way to science, credence in the miraculous intervention of divine forces was being

corroded by the acid of skepticism and overpowered by scientific cosmology.

As Ernst Cassirer succinctly writes (1951; 5): "'Reason' becomes the unifying and central point of this century, expressing all that it longs and strives for, and all that it achieves." This "reason" is essentially the method of natural science. "The procedure is thus not from concepts and axioms to phenomena, but vice versa. Observation produces the datum of science; the principle and law are always the object of the investigation."

> This new methodological order characterizes all eighteenth century thought. (1951; 8)

This victory of the "scientific revolution" privileged method and technology, and also the moral or human sciences. As part of our story on social theory in education, it is important to realize that in the scientific approach to all aspects of life and the beginnings of the human sciences, although it ultimately influences economics and sociology, it is psychology that becomes the defining human science. As Gay writes (1969; 167):

> Not content with making psychology into a science, the Enlightenment made it, among the sciences of man, into the strategic science. It was strategic in offering good, "scientific" grounds for the philosophers' attack on religion; it was strategic in the broader sense of radiating out to other sciences of man, to educational, aesthetic, and political thought—"general psychology."

More recent scholarship on the Enlightenment movement (Outram, 2005) argues for a less unitary and more complex view of the strong, scientific rationalism described by earlier philosophers and historians. She recognizes that later twentieth-century sociologists would identify the Enlightenment with modernity and make it the target of their social criticism. She is referring to the first generation of what is known as the Frankfurt School of critical sociology (2005; 6). But before we bring them into the picture, it important to recognize that that while this movement is historically important for social theory, there is another countermovement against the intellectual and social program of the Enlightenment. That is Romanticism.

Geoffrey Hawthorn, in his book that argues for the Enlightenment influence on the origins of sociology (1976), acknowledges also the relevance of a countermovement(1976):

> Romanticism, after A.W. Schlegel's contemporary definitions is what most have called this extraordinary movement of artistic and intellectual creativity, is inherently difficult to describe. The spiritual and intellectual freedom that it presumed generalized a range of ideas that defy a comprehensive account. It is, perhaps, best characterized as a belief in two propositions: that as one contemporary put it "we live in a world that we ourselves create," and that the principle o creativity is plenitude, infinite variety.

We can already see the contrast to Rationalism, which defines itself precisely in terms of the scientific method in the ambiguity of definition of **Romanticism**.

Romanticism

An intellectual, social movement of the late eighteenth and early nineteenth century expressed in philosophy and literature, especially poetry. Key ideas of this movement include the importance of inner experience, imagination, and creativity. Often considered a countermovement to Enlightenment, Romantic thinkers are vitalistic rather than analytic, oriented to the joy of life and the possibilities of an ongoing renewal of human energy and the reintegration of humanity and society into a dynamic wholeness.

While Romanticism is reflected in the works of philosophers, it is profoundly and clearly also a poetic, literary movement. M.H. Abrams, in his classic study of late eighteenth and early nineteenth-century Romantic poetry, describes it as a "revolutionary" movement. But, it is about an "inner revolution" that occurs in the mind of the individual and in the capacity to experience. If Enlightenment is about reason and analysis, Romanticism is about experience and imagination.

Abrams (1971; 343) describes the inner experiential shift of one poet that he argues characterized Romanticism in general: "the vision of a total and enduring transformation in man and his world; but he shifted the initiative and agency for this transformation from outer revolution to an inner revolution in man's moral, intellectual and imaginative economy." The term he uses to describe the ideals of the poet Wordsworth is "imaginative vision."

This Romantic vision is one of experience, vision, and the possibilities of renewal and rebirth through creative expression. Even more than the ideals of experience as well as imagination, creativity, and joy is the value of life (Abrams, 1971; 431):

> The ground concept is life. Life is itself the highest good, the residence and measure of other goods, and the generator of the controlling categories of Romantic thought...And the norm of life is joy.

A far cry from the importance of empirical observation and an orderly and hierarchical natural world that can be scientifically apprehended.

Sociological Ambivalence

As we describe the three basic models that I believe can organize almost all of our social theorizing and research about education, we will see residues of this countermovement among the classical social theorists as well as in more contemporary theoretical and empirical work. I am suggesting that some of the tensions, contradictions, and ambivalence that we see in the social theory of education is a reflection of a historical cultural conflict between these two movements—Enlightenment versus Romanticism, Reason versus Emotion, Analysis versus Creativity, Elements versus Totality, Structure versus Energy. These are the conflicts that become internalized among the late moderns and the early and ambivalent moderns who formed sociology.

Although these themes appear in both classical and modern sociology, they are often implicit and certainly not traced to specific opposing movements. There is, however, one group of sociologists (and philosophers, and others) who between the time of classical sociology and our own time took up directly a social analysis of the Enlightenment as the flagship of modern culture. That is the Frankfurt School. While we want to say more about their ideas later, as an offshoot of the Marxist model, it is a powerful example of how sociology not only does not originate in modernity but also opposes it.

In their essay "The Concept of Enlightenment" (1972), the leading voices of the Frankfurt School Max Horkheimer and Theodor W. Adorno articulate their sense of betrayal by the modern promise of attaining freedom and human progress through the application of a rational, scientific approach.

We might say colloquially, without any disrespect to their important work, that these are "not happy campers." Keep in mind, of course, that they fled Germany with the rise of Nazism and wrote, we could say, in the shadow of the Holocaust. That is a significant aspect of their social context. Their writing has an almost oral poetic quality to it, in the spirit of Romanticism (1972):

> In the most general sense of progressive thought, the
> Enlightenment has always aimed at liberating men from fear

and establishing their sovereignty. Yet the fully enlightened earth
radiates disaster triumphant.

The last line says it all. Enlightenment and modernity failed. We
are living the disaster. How? (p. 6) "Enlightenment is totalitarian"
(p. 7) and "number became the canon of the Enlightenment"
(p. 9):

> Myth turns into enlightenment, and nature into mere objectivity.
> Men pay for the increase of their power with alienation from
> that over which they exercise their power. Enlightenment behaves
> toward things as a dictator toward men. He knows them in so far
> as he can manipulate them.

As for the power of reason (p. 25):

> Thinking objectifies itself to become an automatic, self-activating
> process; an impersonation of the machine that it produces itself
> so that ultimately the machine can replace it.

I think we get the idea. We moderns, with all of our great hope
for progress and freedom by using the scientific method, have
actually done ourselves in. That is the "dialectic," the internal
dynamic movement, of the Enlightenment.

   The classical social theorists, whose ideas form the basis of
our three models, are, on the whole, less absolutely condemna-
tory of modern society (although Weber can be gloomy). Yet,
I would argue that they too are caught in a dialectic, that is, in
dynamic, internal contradictions and tensions, within their theories. Of course, we could see the up-side, and suggest, as does the
Romantic philosopher Hegel (see Abrams, 1971), that ultimately
they will lead to new and creative syntheses and new unities or to
a re-integration—a view developed by one of his most famous
interpreters and critics, Karl Marx.

   Modern culture, carrying forward Renaissance humanism
(Toulmin, 1990) as well as the Enlightenment, is individualistic.
Yet, it also continues to express a longing for the value of non-
individualistic commitments. For example, we will see in the work
of Durkheim, how, as society develops, so does individualism. So
much so, that Durkheim is working against the grain of too much
individualism. He values individualism and the civil, republica-
tion society based on individual human rights. Indeed, when he
tries to find a path to control the costs and dangers of excessive

individualism, by bringing in shared social rituals as the social-izing, balancing factor, he builds society around the individual. The religion of the future, as a way out of hyper-individualism, is to venerate individualism, but in a social way, to make a religion of the individual. He calls it "the cult of the individual."

While most commentators would say that Durkheim was a very strict rationalist, founding a "science" of sociology, he brings back forms of life that precede modern individualism in order to make society work. Not only with Durkheim but, as we shall see, even among late modern or postmodern thinkers such as Manuel Castells, there is a recognition that the continuing development of the separate individual calls forth reactions and expresses the need for social attachment and belonging.

I would call this "the return of the social." Repeatedly, in Marx and Weber as well as in Durkheim and in other modern social thinkers as well, alongside documentation and encourage-ment and approval for the development of the individual, there is a quest to find something more basic and more deeply engaging that can express human community, belonging, and solidarity. If the aspiration of modern culture is to attain individual freedom by removing the shackles and bonds of tradition, convention, and social constraint, then, at the same time, there is a gnawing search for what Abrams (1971) sees as a hallmark of Romanticism: reintegration, bringing the parts back into a unified whole. If the Enlightenment wanted the dissecting, separating, if not fragment-ing, aspect of an analytical way of life, Romanticism quests for its antidote: reunifying all that has been separated. In this sense, the tension between the individual and society—an enduring theme of social theory—is also part of its cultural modern context and of its two-sidedness and ambivalence.

So too with science. Marx begins with the Romantic phi-losophy of Hegel and moves in the course of his work, through admiration for Darwin and British economics, increasingly toward a more law-like, empirical scientific approach to social analysis. Perhaps, returning to early Enlightenment influences, in the best spirit of that era and its philosophical commitments, Marx privileges technology. It is technology, the embodiment of human scientific reason, that moves humanity forward through the course of social history. Technology is the progressive force that ultimately determines so much of the rest of our lives. But, technology is embedded and even, we could say, contextualized in the nonscientific, human social bonds of those who create, produce, and activate it. These social relations are not set by technology, but by the way that people organize themselves socially, by design, by force, and by conditions inherited from the past, by tradition. Scientific reason cannot fully free itself from history and from human interconnection and traditional forms of relating.

In fact, Marx, as we shall see in elaborating his model of social theory, makes this tension explicit—though, not as between Enlightenment and Romanticism, or between the modern and the premodern. The cultural tension and ambivalence of modernity is presented as itself a law of the science of society, as a generalization. That generalization is that the main conflict in the organization of society that leads to the conflict of social groups, especially social classes, is between always advancing technology and a lagging set of social relations. Marx works brilliantly with this tension, to create a dynamic theory of society. But the tension itself, I suggest, is not only one of a universal, general social law, but of the context of modernity in which Marx lived and wrote. There can be a social basis to ideas, including ideas in conflict, even among those who recognize the social context as informing social theory. We recall that this is one of the "tricky" aspects of having a sociology of knowledge understanding of social theory.

The cultural and social context of modernity in everyday life and in social theory is not unitary, but conflicted and ambivalent. If, for simplicity sake, we locate the individual-social tension in Durkheim's theory, and the scientific-relational/traditional tension in Marx, then Weber is arguably the best example of the tension between the rational on the one side, and the emotional and spiritual on the other.

We recall that even in the complexity of the historical scholarship about the Enlightenment, there is broad agreement that this intellectual movement advanced science and reason against core aspects of religious belief and faith. Indeed, if there is any argument and a suggestion that some aspects of religion might have been supported and continued, there is a general agreement that the more mystical, emotional, spiritual aspects of religion were to be replaced by rationality.

Weber is most famous as the social chronicler of the rise of bureaucracy in the modern world. Bureaucracy, as a type of

social organization, is based on the principle of rationality. In the social logic of rationality, action is decided upon and has value and authority to the extent that it follows rules and laws. Ideally, the rules ought to bring efficient results, enabling us to achieve our ends by the most effective means. Weber is a self-conscious analyst of modern culture. He sees himself as a product of this culture or "civilization." He is self-aware also in that he sees his role as analytical and wants to refrain from making value judgments about his social world. Of course, he recognized that he cannot completely refrain. Indeed, the tension between the triumph of reason as the organizational principle of rationality, of laws, of calculation for efficiency, and the non-rational, emotional, religious, and spiritual becomes the cornerstone of Weber's social theory. He shows us how to analyze bureaucracy and he recognizes that calculation according to rules can bring efficiency. Yet, he does not like it.

How did we get into this place, where rules and calculation make us less personal, less human, less spiritual, less able to give meaning to our lives? That is Weber's question. That is the question about modern culture. And, most importantly, that is the question to which he does indeed provide at least one very scholarly answer in the development of his social theory. We will unfold this third ambivalence of modernity, between the rational and the spiritual, when we describe Weber's social theory and the Weberian tradition and its implications for education. As an introductory hint, we can say now and maybe already guess that if Durkheim brings back the social to moderate the individual, and Marx brings in traditional human forms of social relations as the opposing tension of scientific technology, then Weber returns religion, against the long secularizing trend of modern Western European culture, to society. We should note cautiously, at the outset, that however prominent the history of spiritual and emotional religiosity may be in Weber's social theory, in real life, both for the social future and for himself, he is not very optimistic about its success.

Characters

I am reluctant to delve too much into the personal lives or our theorists, because our "story" here is a story about analytical models of classical social theory and how they continue to structure what we know, think, and research about education, form a social point of view. Similarly, I have offered only some limited description and, hopefully, insight about the intellectual, cultural, and social context of social theory, because we need to keep to our story line. On the other hand, as we have seen, the context does make a difference to the content, although we surely would not want to reduce it to that. So too, with the lives of our main protagonists, the embodied lives of the creators of our story, its main biographical characters. Indeed, following Mills' (1959) idea that the sociological imagination makes the connection between individual biography and social history, we can perhaps benefit from a brief tour of the lives of the characters who first wrote the story of major trends in classical social theory.

Robert Bellah (1973), who is, in my view, a leading interpreter of Durkheim and the Durkheimian tradition, writes about Durkheim's life, in this way (1973; xi)

> Emile Durkheim was born on 15 April 1858, in Epinal, a French speaking town in the Vosges near the Alsace border. His father was Moise Durkheim, a rabbi, who became Grand Rabbi of the Vosges. It was intended that Emile become a rabbi in accordance with family tradition, and he studied Hebrew in his youth.

Bellah continues:

> The social context in which Durkheim came to define his life work was decisively affected when he was twelve years old by the crushing defeat of France by Germany in the War of 1870, and by the subsequent fall of the Second Empire and establishment of the Third French Republic.

Durkheim wanted to "play a role in the social reconstitution of a France wounded in defeat." We see in Durkheim's early formation, the importance of both religion and nationalism. At the same time, almost every account of his life and work describes Durkheim as a "rationalist." His own highest commitments were to rationality, science, and humanity and to French society insofar as it embodied these ideal. From his youth in the peripheral provinces, Durkheim succeeded in the French national exam system to gain entrance to the prestigious Ecole normale superiure in Paris. He had a successful academic career, first as a professor of Pedagogy and later, as professor of Pedagogy and Sociology. Durkheim was the first professor of Sociology in France, and it

is interesting from our point of view that he began in Education and combined the two fields. Indeed, he taught teachers and wrote on educational topics throughout his life. If religion helps constitute society, education transmits its moral integration to the next generation.

The way in which the rationalist aspect of modern culture is embodied in Durkheim's life and career is also noted by Hawthorn's account of him (1976; 116):

> He entered the Ecole Normal Superiure in 1879, where he was remembered for his republican enthusiasm and his distaste for what he regarded as the frivolous dilettantism or sheer mysticism of much of the teaching. He appears to have been a morally serious young man, and to have adopted the cause of republican nationalism with all the fervour of a convert to Parisian intellectual life. His ideological convictions together with his moral seriousness inclined him to a faith in intellectual rigour, in the virtues of an uncompromising rationalism and a nominal empiricism in the French manner.

Various biographical accounts relay anecdotes about his intellectual seriousness and moral demeanor as well as about his commitment to creating a viable liberal civil society in France. He wrote on current political and social topics and authored a series of now classic works in academic social theory. He is widely considered the founder of modern sociology, although the term was used by earlier French theorists. Durkheim, however, helped to institutionalize sociology in France, not only as its first professor, but also as founding editor of the journal *L'Annee Sociologique* (the Sociological Annual).

The rationalism and scientific orientation attributed to Durkheim is, of course, expressed in his methodological assertions of sociology as a science and in his empirical and theoretical works that try to describe social facts and develop laws of social life. Yet, in Durkheim, along with what we have been calling the Enlightenment rationalism, we find an emotionally strong nationalism and, perhaps less evidently, in his adult life, the influences not only of Judaism in general, but of the particular style of Judaism that he learned at home.

We can see, I think, his personal quest for societal rebuilding in the central role that the question of solidarity (and later, of social energy) plays in Durkheim's theory. Reconstituting—or we might even say, as Abrams described Romanticism, reintegrating—society is a theme that he takes as a "mission" (Bellah, 1973). In practice and, importantly, in theory as well. Durkheim's theoretical work, which, of all our classical "characters," has had the most influence on mainstream sociology, represents an effort to discover how this integration can be accomplished. Individualism is not adequate to the task, and so, he turns to what he eventually sees as the basic form of the social—religion. Religion provides the basic model of social life, Durkheim argues. Religion is the core social activity that creates the energy and forms social solidarity and integration. It is the "elementary form" of the social, the source of social ideas and social attachments.

The irony of Durkheim's rationalism and nationalism and his individualism is that he looks toward the premodern forms of association, namely, the dynamic energy of religious gatherings as the basis of social integration. The ideas of morality itself are generated in the course of collective ritual assemblies, organized around religious symbols. The secular professor of what has been called the "civil religion" (Bellah, 1973) that Durkheim wanted to design for France, finds the deep source of social being and integration in religious practice.

The irony of Durkheim's rationalism and individualism—in the methodology and content of his wok, against this background of the premodern source of society in religious rituals—gets even more interesting, if we return to the biographical question of Durkheim's own religion, his Jewishness. Here, the conventional wisdom is that Durkheim's commitment to science and rationalism comes not only from the Enlightenment tradition, but also from his Jewish origins. Strenski (1997; 58) reviews the scholarly literature concerning the influence of the religious factor on Durkheim's thought:

> At any rate, Louis M. Greenberg has argued that the tendencies of Durkheim's rationalist Talmudic father discouraged indulgence in the arts, mysticism, or poetry—an attitude that certainly typifies Durkheim's adult opinions...Greenberg argues that Moise Durkheim's devotion to the puritanical and rationalist bent of Rashi's Talmudic school of Troyes, derailed such attractions.

He goes on to cite additional commentators:

> Derczansky has urged us to see Durkheim's moral rigorism, Puritanism, and resistance to social revolution as indicators of Durkheim's formation in the antimystical, antimessianic spirit of

the Talmudic Judaism of the Troyes Talmudic school, in which Durkheim's father was educated.

Ivan Strenski (1997) rejects these arguments from early influence on theoretical content. Instead, he suggests, Durkheim was influenced by his colleagues at the Ecole Pratiques des Hautes Etudes in Paris, who in the study of both Judaism and Hinduism emphasized the importance of social rituals as the core of religious life. Not paternal, but professional, influence matters. Strenski (1997; 147) writes, of this view:

> Ritual is the locus of the positive power of the sacred that injects effervescence, energy and power into people and that causes people to be religious at all.

Whichever interpretation of the connection between Durkheim's historical social context, his biography, and his social theory we accept, we can see the tensions in his work between the individual and society and between the rational and the sacred. How these tensions play out in the work of explaining education socially, and in the tradition of social understanding that he founded, we shall see in our "story" of the Durkheimian model.

If we wish to find in Emile Durkheim's biography the roots of the theoretical importance that he attaches to achieving social integration and to the importance of religious ritual in generating the ideas and energy for this solidarity, we can find in Marx's biography the personal roots of quite a different theoretical emphasis. David McLellan (1973), in his authoritative work on the life and thought of Karl Marx, opens his account by underlining just such a correspondence between Marx's biography and his theory. It is worth quoting (1973; 1):

> It may seem paradoxical that Karl Marx, whom so many working-class movements of our time claim as their Master and infallible guide to revolution, should have come from a comfortable middle-class home. Yet to a remarkable extent he does himself epitomize his own doctrine that men are conditioned by their socio-economic circumstances. The German city in which he grew up have him a sense of long historical tradition and at the same time close contact with the grim realities of the underdevelopment then characteristic of Germany. Thoroughly Jewish in their origins, Protestant by necessity yet living in a Catholic region, his family could never regard their social integration as

complete. The sense of alienation was heightened in Marx's personal case by his subsequent inability to obtain teaching post in a university system that had no room for dissident intellectuals.

Marx was born in Trier on 5 May 1818. A community of about 15,000 inhabitants, it was the oldest city in Germany, also one of the loveliest.

Surely, although Marx's grandparents were Jewish, religion played a less important role in his family life than in Durkheim's. Eleanor, Marx's daughter, recalls of her grandfather: (McLellan 1973; 6)

> "he was steeped in the free French ideas of the eighteenth century on politics, religion, life and art." He subscribed entirely to the views of the eighteenth century French rationalists, sharing their limitless faith in the power of reason to explain and improve the world.

Marx's father was secular and liberal and he actively involved in public political life. Marx himself was the only founder of classical sociology who was not a professional academic, Marx had earned a doctoral degree and was a candidate for a university position. But his patrons and their political views were unacceptable to the narrow confines of the traditional German university of his times. He became a journalist and an editor, first in Germany and then later in Paris and Brussels. Marx was a political activist as well and was often pursued by local authorities with warrants issued for his arrest. The newspapers and yearbooks that he wrote for were repeatedly censored by the authorities in Germany as well as in the other countries to which Marx and his family fled as political exiles.

Randall Collins describes Marx's intellectual, professionally marginal position in this rather positive way (1994; 40):

> Another role-hybrid, as we have already seen is Marx, who would likely have been a notable philosophy professor if he had not been forced out of the university by political circumstances. He made up for it by creating a comprehensive general theory out of his revolutionary ideas.

As a "role-hybrid"—part academic, part journalist, part political activist—Marx developed his theory partly in dialogue with the work of G.W. Hegel (the great German philosopher of his time) and the school of theorists who engaged and worked to modify Hegel's theory of history that Marx made famous as one

of the "Young Hegelians." These included not only intellectual colleagues and disputants, but also close friends and political comrades. Marx was, almost until his last decade, involved with political organizations that aimed to articulate and actualize a variety of socialist and communist ideals. If Durkheim was influenced by the defeat of France in the War of 1870, Marx was witness to the workers' revolutions of 1848 that occurred across Europe, but especially in France. As McLellan observes of Marx's final exile in England, and his earlier revolutionary experience (1973; 226):

> When Marx came to England certainly he had no idea that he would make it his permanent home. For years he shared the view of most of his fellow refugees that a new round of revolutions would soon break out on the Continent. Like the early Christians awaiting the Second Coming, they regarded their present life as of little importance compared to the great event that was to come.

Marx's theory represents this revolutionary hope as an inevitable result of the logic of history, driven, we recall, by the endlessly progressive force of technological dynamism. The power of collective action and the sociality of class politics are what Marx observed in the practice of the French socialists and the immigrant German workers parties (in McLellan, 1973; 87):

> when French socialist workers meet together. Smoking, eating and drinking are no longer simply means of bringing people together. Company, association, entertainment which also has society as its aim, are sufficient for them; the brotherhood of man is no empty phrase but a reality, and the nobility of man shines forth upon us from their toil-worn bodies.

Nor was Marx an economically comfortable observer of poverty and financial suffering. Despite his middle-class origins, his biography is replete with descriptions of situations of dire and apparently endless poverty that caused his own and his family's suffering. In a letter, Marx describes one of the many episodes in his continual poverty (in McLellan, 1973; 263):

> You will certainly b able appreciate the humour of the book when you consider that its author, through lack of sufficient covering for his back and feet, is a good as interned and also was and

is threatened with seeing really nauseating poverty overwhelm his family at any moment.

We see in Marx's own life history the unavoidable importance of the economic factor. Of course, his theory of society that begins within the Romantic tradition and its quest for reintegration—that Marx developed in his early work on alienation—moves increasingly to an economic, production, and technological determination of the scientific laws of social life. At the same time, the camaraderie and solidarity that Marx observed in the workers movements give at least an experiential basis to his more abstract theories of how revolutions are made when people in the same socioeconomic situation begin to consolidate and form a common social awareness. Even his exile from Germany and his impoverished uprooting of his family to avoid the censors and the police could be seen reflected in the international character of the theoretical traditions that feed into Marx's grand scheme. In parallel, Marx's political organizing activity was also internationalized, as the workers' movements fused into an International, the practical organizational embodiment of Marx's hopes for world revolution. Sometimes, the practical and the theoretical conflicted in the life of this intellectual/activist hybrid. "One of the main reasons why volume One of Capital was so long in appearing and why the subsequent volumes never appeared at all is that Marx's time was taken up by the work forced on him as the leading figure of the International (McLellan, 1973; 360).

If we find in Durkheim's life some existential roots of the theoretical importance that he gives to social integration and religion, and if we find in Marx's experiences simultaneously the suffering of poverty and the importance of the economic factor, as well as the hope in revolutionary forms of association that are reminiscent of the premodern social lives of worker, then, with Weber, we find the ambivalence and contradiction of modernity itself.

In their well-known collection of translations and selections from the sociology of Max Weber, Hans Gerth and C. Mills offer their "biographical view." They begin (1946; 3):

> Max Weber was born in Erfurt, Thuringia, on 21 April, 1864.
> His father, Max Weber Sr., a trained jurist and municipal counselor, came from a family of linen merchants and textile manufacturers of western Germany. In 1869 the Webers moved to Berlin,

which was soon to become the booming capital of Bismarck's Reich. There, Weber Sr. became a prosperous politician, active in the municipal die of Berlin, the Prussian diet, and the New Reichstag. He belonged to the right-wing liberals.

Of Weber's mother, they simply note: "Max Weber's mother, Helene Fallenstein Weber, was a cultured and liberal woman of Protestant faith."

Max Weber himself did his doctoral dissertation in law and political economy and became a successful young academic. In 1897, however, by all accounts, Weber expressed hostility against his father, intervening in an argument between his parents and defending his mother. Weber later fell sick; whether, as is usually suggested in accounts of Weber's life (see Mitzman, 1969), it was because of this familial encounter or because of his strenuous academic work habits is a matter of conjecture. Gerth and Mills describe this episode (1946; 11):

> During the following summer, the Webers traveled to Spain and on the return trip Weber became fevered and ill with a psychic malady...towards the end of the fall semester he collapsed from tension and remorse, exhaustion and anxiety.

For the rest of his life he suffered intermittently from severe depressions, punctuated by manic spurts of extraordinarily intense intellectual work and travel. Only toward the end of his life, and even then, only briefly, would he fulfill the responsibilities of a full-time academic, university professor.

It is difficult to avoid the importance of the family drama in the life of this complex man and one of our core classical sociologist. Yet, we should also try to see the biography and the family drama together in the broader social and cultural context of his times. I want to suggest that we see the parental conflict as symbolic of a deeper cultural conflict. Moreover, I think it is precisely this conflict, whether in the family or in the wider sociocultural level, that serves Weber as the axis for his analyses of historical social and cultural change.

Weber's mother was apparently a central figure in Max Weber's life, and he remained close to her, corresponding in intimate letters, until her death. Taking her side, as it were, in the family conflict is perhaps in some way later articulated in Weber's theory. For his mother was a deeply religious person who originated and lived in a network of serious religious thought. His father was a public figure and, like Weber at the beginning of his career, a lawyer. We don't want to amateurishly "psychoanalyze" Weber, although Mitzman (1969) offers an intriguing psychohistory that links the development of Weber's ideas to his personal development. Nevertheless, it is not a big jump to see the social theoretical representation between the legal (Weber wrote about rational authority as the "rational legal") and the spiritual and emotional. Of course, it is more than that, since Weber was trying to understand the historical development of modern European culture and society and did prodigious comparative social analyses in order to understand the particular nature of modern European culture.

Yet, there is a nagging parallel between the family dynamic and the theoretical dynamic. At the heart of Weber's theory of society is an effort to understand why the rational (the rational-legal) has prevailed in society, against both tradition and spiritual life. The answer that he develops is that the rational begins in the spiritual, in magic, in emotionality, in feeling and ecstasy, in the highly personal power that he calls "charisma." But charisma, as we shall see in our account of the Weberian tradition, is a term taken from religion. The core conflict of modern society is between these two ways of being, the rational and the spiritual. Rationality wins, but at a price. The price is the loss of personal relation, of feeling and sensuality, and ultimately of the spirit and the meaning of life. Life becomes rationalized. Bureaucracy is only its most evident organizational form. Religion is betrayed by the need to intellectualize and abstract, and so it stops being magical and becomes rational. Occasionally, charisma bursts out, breaking the power of rational domination. Still the future is not rosy, since charisma is always brought back into the fold, routinized, losing its magical power. His reconciliation of the cultures of Enlightenment and Romanticism does not have a clearly happy ending.

Still, we shall see how this conflict works out, and why Weber is the theorist not only of the social or the economic but of the cultural as well. For in his work (and we can say fairly, I think, in his life), Weber is on a different quest than the other giants of classical sociology. Not social solidarity or economic justice, but meaning itself is the aim of Weber's social theory.

The intersection of biography and history can be endlessly fascinating. Making the connections between social and intellectual contexts and social theories is an engaging and important task. But, for social theorists, the proof is always in the pudding. Our question is whether the theory helps us to better understand social life, and, for us, in this book, especially the social process of education. The theoretical giants of classical social theory, about whom we have now had a contextual and biographical glimpse, live on, not by virtue of their personal magnetism or interesting lives. Their immortality is in the creative power they displayed, using their lives and environment as cultural resources for the creation of theoretical understanding. It is the theory that lives on, and it lives on because it speaks to us now, across the life and times of its creators.

Let's see now if it speaks to you and helps make better sense of education as a social process. We begin then, with an overview of the three models.

Three Models

The models of social process that are represented in the classical tradition express different ideas about what is important in society, about how social relations work, and how societies remain stable and change. Yet, what the theories or models have in common is that they express the culture of modernity, along with its contradictions. We would say that they work within the **"problematic"** of modernity. Part of what that means is that in each of the three traditions/theories/models, general social problems are taken as questions to be explained systematically, by using interrelated sets of concepts or theories. Classical sociology takes to the problems of the modern era, notably those of the late nineteenth and early twentieth century, by setting out broader analytical questions around which it develops systematic attempts or theories to explain the nature and workings of these problems. Each model within the tradition emphasizes different aspects or problems within the culture of the modern social world.

The theories also have in common that although they are conscious efforts to develop coherent understandings of social life, there is also tension and even contradiction within each of the theories. Although this book is a short introduction

Problematic

Refers to the package of questions asked regarding both social problems of the context and the concepts that comprise the models of explanation.

to the topic, it would be foolhardy for us to confuse "intro-duction" with stereotype and oversimplification. We know that life is complex and full of tensions and contradictions. So are social theories, even when they aim for coherence and for a holistic grasp of the meaning of society and social processes. It is valuable to balance the drive for coherence and holistic under-standing with a counterbalancing recognition of complexity, tension, and contradiction—in the same way that we understand simultaneously both the contextual origins of social theories as well as their trans-contextual more general import for analyzing social life.

The third characteristic that these theories have in common is their enduring nature. They are "classical" not only in that they were foundational for different streams of sociological thinking, but also because they continue to influence theory and research in sociology and in many other fields, including Education—when we are prepared to think about Education socially.

The durability of these theories is the reason why we can talk about them as models. The basic ideas of each theory can be seen in long traditions of social analyses of education continuing into the present. Classical sociology sets the framework for social interpretations of all stripes, and for empirical research done with different methodologies. Although not everyone would agree about the durability and frame-setting importance of these theories, I think we can show how foundational, classical social theory, in its aim for a holistic, coherent social understanding, and despite the tensions within each theory, has constituted a set of traditions of social analysis. We can see how each of the theories works itself out in the way that education was thought socially over the course of many years and into the present and in various places. Social theory in education is not only classical sociology. It also encom-passes various contemporary postmodern theories and research studies. But, its concepts are so powerful that they continue to organize our thinking about education as a social process. That is why we can talk about "models," as sets of coherent concepts aimed at description and analysis, in relation to classical sociology. The early, modern, foundational theories of the most influential classical social analysts have continued to provide the basic ideas through which we do our own social analyses of education. What are they?

Durkheim, Marx, and Weber—Society, Economy, and Culture

Durkheim

There are a number of possible ways to give an overview of each model. In sociology of education, it is commonplace to describe the tradition of social theory that begins with Durkheim as "Functionalism" and to juxtapose it to the enormous range of works in the tradition that begins with Marx and to call that "Conflict." Regrettably, the tradition of social theory that has implications for Education and that begins with Weber is ordinarily absent.

I have sometimes grouped the founding theorists—the social theorists of education who continue his ideas and the research that exemplifies them—into three categories. Durkheim is the starting point for thinking about education in relation to basic social processes of **integration**. That is close to the Functionalist interest in how social institutions work in relation to maintaining the stability of the whole society. The most famous Functionalists are placed under Durkheim's umbrella. But, that is only part of the story. It is not only that Durkheim is also interested in change. Rather it is also that stability and the **reproduction** of existing societies are secondary to the creation of sociality, of the "togetherness" that is the core of social integration, which is a condition of social continuity.

I am going to bring up some of Durkheim's own writings, or at least a small glimmer of them, so that we can see how the real question for him is how society is created in the first place, how social integration, cohesion, or togetherness is created in social processes. We will then see by both theoretical and research examples how this interest is carried along in contemporary social theory in education. We can already hint, even at this point, that the social problem and the analytical problematic are linked for Durkheim. His social worry was that the development of individualism as part of the social world of modernity had gone so far that the very processes that make society in the first place and that create sociality are at risk of dissolving. While he worried about too much individualism, he also appreciated the modern valuation of the individual and his sociopolitical status as a citizen within a republic. Among the tensions that we mentioned, in

Integration
Durkheim's term to describe how society holds together. When there is a lack of shared symbols, social coordination, and a sense of common belonging, people suffer from a lack of moral regulation. "Anomie" is the unhappy result of a lack of social integration.

Reproduction
As a general term, refers to replication. While in early Marxist theory the emphasis is on the replication of workers and their life conditions, later it comes to mean the way that culture serves to replicate and continue the existing structure of society.

Durkheim there is the ongoing real world and theoretical struggle between the demands of the collective and of the individual.

The concept of "integration" indicates the solution of the struggle, but not its process. That process is the social itself, the coming together of people in groups, their sharing of common symbols, and their generation of shared social energy and cultural meanings in general and of morality in particular, through coordinated social interactions or rituals. Religious rituals are formative, according to Durkheim, but they are also the paradigm for secular, nonreligious rituals. What is important is the process of assembling, sharing, interacting, and co-creating, in an organized synchronous way, the morally regulative social order without which both collectivities and individuals are weakened and disorganized and thus eventually collapse and disintegrate.

For this reason, although he had deep cultural interests and saw the economic as integral to the development and change of whole societies, I want to think of Durkheim as the theorist of the social. The various faces of Durkheim's social—the ritual assemblies, the co-creation of shared ideas and moral commitments, and the perpetuation of a meaningful and non-chaotic collective life—all have implications for how we understand, research, and practice education.

Marx

There are different streams of intellectual work in both social understanding in general and in education that can be traced to Durkheim. This is part of the complexity and tension that exists not only in his own work, but also in the work of his "heirs," although, despite their differences, they would still identify with the Durkheimian tradition.

Marx's work is even vaster and, arguably, more complex. We can find differences within it, between the early and later works, and when we survey his corpus of work as a whole. Yet, I would suggest that the tradition of Marxist theory is even more heterogeneous and contradictory than the Durkheimian tradition. No doubt this is in part because Marx's theory serves as a conceptual foundation for an enduring tradition of theory and research not only about society, but—in recent years, despite Marx's own relatively scant attention to the question—also about Education.

Rather, the complexity and contentiousness come about from the deep way that Marxist theory is openly bound up with a history of practical social movements and has been so profoundly a part of world politics in the past century and a half. The history of Marxism is at once a political and a social history that is much wider and more variegated than the tradition of Marxist theory (Marx and Engels, 1959). That theoretical tradition is hardly simple and unified either. There are many different and even opposing faces and voices that claim Marx as their common theoretical and political ancestor.

Although Marx was a philosopher, political activist, and journalist, his focus on explaining social life (Bottomore and Rubel, 1956) and his great influence on social thought qualify him as one of the giants of classical sociology. While beginning to write about the years almost a half century before Durkheim and ultimately, overlapping some, I consider that like Durkheim, his "problematic" also grows in the soil of the emerging culture of modernity. As with Durkheim's theory, it is possible to trace the various intellectual streams of thought that fed into Marx's original synthesis. That puts the founders of theoretical traditions themselves into older traditions that influenced them.

Our approach though is to put more emphasis, at the start, on the context of modern culture. The traditions of classical sociology are different from each other because they build upon different concepts and because they have spawned different enduring traditions of theory and research about society and education. They are different in their very foundations also because they see different aspects of their own historical social context as profoundly problematic, as causing individual suffering that, for sociologists (Mills, 1959; Gouldner, 1970; Lemert, 1995), is due to the specific nature of the societies in which they live.

Marx is a sociologist in the classical tradition not only because he created a system of interrelated concepts that work as a model for interpreting social processes. More importantly, he identified the social problems of his times that were interwoven with his basic concepts and tried to explain them, socially as well as to provide a model of social practice that is seen to follow from the theory.

It is too simple to say that Durkheim is the social theorist of the "social" and that Marx is the social theorist of the "economic." But it is true that they saw the pressing problems of modern society and culture differently and that they used different concepts to try to explain and point the way toward practical solutions of these problems. For Marx, the historical evolution of societies is less bound up with the forms of social integration and the types of ritual gatherings in a society, and more directly connected to the way that work or "**production**" is organized: the way people "produce their lives," the everyday material needs of sustenance. These ways of working or producing what we need to sustain ourselves are socially organized.

Production

As a general term, refers to replication. While in early Marxist theory the emphasis is on the replication of workers and their life conditions, later it comes to mean the way that culture serves to replicate and continue the existing structure of society.

We can think of this emphasis on production as economic because, although it is socially patterned, it is about work and material production, and one of its most basic driving elements is technology. We may say that his theory of society is economic because it puts production first (McLennan, 2000). But we should realize that it is economic in a social way. Marx's economic vision of the social is not one of a marketplace collection of separate individuals who are all working and selling and buying. Rather, the economic is organized and patterned in a particular collective way that shapes the lives of individuals and groups far beyond their actual work and narrowly economic activity.

Class

In Marx's theory, the position of people in relation to their ownership of the means of production, of who controls labor and its fruits. In capitalist societies, there are two main and opposing classes: the owners (who are the capitalist class) and the proletariat (who are workers).

Economic production is a social process. I hope that we shall see later how the character of production influences and fits in with all of the social processes in any society, especially what it means for modern society. Questions of "**class**" and "**ideology**" and "reproduction" that have become central in the application of the Marxist tradition of social theory to Education are all rooted in the primacy that Marx accords to economic production as shaping the organization of society and the lives of individuals.

Ideology

Marx's term, taken from the history of French revolutionary thought, to describe how social class position and interests shape and distort thinking and ideas.

Historically, there have always been problems that originate in the social process of producing the material needs of everyday life. Marx was especially interested in the modern problems, in the social life problems caused by the changes in production that created a particular kind of society that he called "capitalist." Technically, capitalism is a mode of production, but it effects social relations beyond the production process itself. Still, we can see why in an important sense it is reasonable to think of Marx's theory as "economic." The social problems of the modern capitalist society are problems that we now identify and conceptualize

generally and that reappear in Marxist social analyses of education as problems of power and of inequality.

"**Alienation**" (Ollman, 1970) is a Marxian term taken from philosophy and used to shed light on a core problem of the social economy of modern capitalism. Capitalism is a social organization of modern production that takes creative power and capacity away from people who actually produce the wealth of society. In this society, people who do most of the productive work do not have real control or power in making decisions about what is being produced, how it is being produced, or what happens to finished products. Their power, which is the power to work and to create these products, is taken away or "alienated" from them. The other main social problem with modern capitalism is "**exploitation**," which, like alienation, is not a historically novel problem but one that is intensified in Marx's time. The economic value that people create when they work is only in part returned to them. The taking away or appropriation of the value of products by others is part and parcel of the division of society into social classes, into workers and capitalists The roots of the conflict between social groups can be found in alienation and exploitation.

There are many differences, tensions, and contradictions within the tradition of Marxist theory. For some theorists, including those working on education as a social process, the importance of the economic or "production determinism" (McLennan, 2000) continues to influence how they understood society and education (Bowles and Gintis, 1976). Others want to make the cultural side of Marxism more relevant (Willis, 1977). Perhaps the greatest tension in this tradition of classical social theory begins with Marx himself. He wanted to underline the power of people, especially when consciously organized around their common economic and social positions and interests, to affect their own lives and to shape the social future. At the same time, he insisted on the power of the social organization or the structure of social production to determine the course of people's individual lives and of their shared futures. "People make their own history," he wrote (Marx, 1956; 320), "but they do not make it just as they please; they do not make it under circumstances chosen by themselves, but under circumstances directly encountered, given and transmitted from the past." There is a tension in Marxist social theory between, on the

---

Alienation

Marx's term for the loss of one's creative power and control over work and the products of work, a loss that results from the particular way that work is organized in capitalism.

Exploitation

Marx's term for the result of the work process in which the value or wealth that the proletariat creates is returned to them only partially. Most of the wealth that their work creates is taken by the capitalist class.

one hand, a social structure that determines individual and group actions and, on the other, the possibilities of individual and collective social action—conscious action and social movements that can change the structure itself.

These social problems and theoretical tensions continue to be expressed in the work of social theorists and researchers in Education who are influenced by the tradition of Marxist social theory. They have been called "new sociologists of education," "neo-Marxists," and "radicals" (Wexler, 2007a). Whatever the name, Marx is the founding and formative source of the second of our three models of social theory in education.

Weber

The reason why Weber is sometimes thought of as being a corrective to Marx is his emphasis on the importance of ideas for shaping society. It is more accurate to say that Weber had a "multi-causal" view of the forces determining social life. For this reason, he is also thought of as the first "postmodern" social theorist (Gane, 2005) since he had a less unified/coherent and more multiplex view of social processes.

Our ideas of Marx's economic and Durkheim's social were acknowledged by Weber. But, social organization and integration as well as economic production and work also needed to be seen within and alongside the development of ideas and beliefs in the history of societies. For Weber, who saw himself as a modern, European person (despite his more postmodern, contemporary emphasis on multiplicity), what had to be understood was the importance of religious ideas in setting the framework of modern society, even after that society had become more secular.

Indeed, he is most famous for his study of how the religious ideas of the Protestant Reformation came to affect the everyday actions and psychology, the dispositions or "**habitus**," of the people who created modern capitalism. Capitalism is not only an organization of economic production or an integrated social system, but also a way of thinking and feeling about the world, about specific beliefs and motivations. Capitalism is a culture. Weber tried to show how religious ideas, the "Protestant Ethic," unintentionally came to operate as a culture in the everyday lives of the people who first formed and perpetuated modern capitalist

---

Habitus

Weber's way of describing the intersection of culture and psychology. Character types, like the self-denying or ascetic Protestant, are an example of how a culture comes to work in the everyday life of people. Bourdieu later expanded this idea, writing about dispositions and about unspoken internalized rules for action that come from the context.

society. Religious beliefs or ethics thus generated a "spirit" of capitalism (Weber, 1958).

This conceptual emphasis on the importance of beliefs that become embedded in people's motivations, of a religious ethic that becomes an economic and social spirit, makes the theoretical point that culture is part of the explanation of social processes. But, like the other foundational theorists, Weber was not only himself influenced by the modern culture context of his times but was also a critic of it. And as in the case of the other "giants," his social criticism is interwoven with his basic concepts and takes the direction of the theoretical tradition that he helped to establish. The social problem that is a kind of central pivot for Weber's theories is the problem of modern culture. Modern culture is a secular culture. When it evolved from a religious culture that had been so important in human history, although something may have been gained for society, something else was lost. What was gained was the replacement of magical thinking by rational thought, calculation, and planning that led to greater efficiency in society. Weber is the social theorist of **bureaucracy**, which is a form of social organization that best represents the development of a modern culture of rationality. The rational core of the culture, like Marx's capitalism in work and production, spreads out to all aspects of the society. Everything becomes more consciously calculated, planned, and organized as to whether it is the most efficient means to achieve cultural goals or ends.

The problem is that the means become the ends. All social process is rationalization. Bureaucracy triumphs. Religion, especially its magical spirit, disappears and societies become emptied of mystery. Old-fashioned personalism and doing things by way of tradition disappears too, along with the magical elements that Weber called "**charisma**." Instead of tradition and charisma, we have rules, calculations, and laws, what he called the authority of the "rational-legal" that demands obedience (Weber, 1968).

The tensions in Weber's theory have to do with this constellation of ideas about religion, capitalism, and bureaucracy. On the one hand, Weber wants us to be very careful about our use of concepts and scientific in our research methodology. He rails against university teachers who try to use the classroom as a place to express their own political commitments and talks about "value-neutrality" in science (Gerth and Mills, 1946). At

Bureaucracy

Weber's term for a particular type of social organization where rational calculation and set rules prevail and where the goal is to m aximize efficiency. Here, social action is organized in terms of rational and legal rules, rather than either tradition or charisma.

Charisma

Weber's terms, taken from Christian theology, meaning "grace." Weber uses it to refer to the extraordinary power and magnetism of historical individuals that leads people to willingly obey them. Charisma begins in magical power and stands opposed to rationality and bureaucracy.

the same time, he laments the loss of magic, of a more personal style in social life, and the mechanical and impersonal nature of a modern culture of "experts." He is torn between a desire for objectivity and for moral commitment and a social criticism of modern culture.

The importance of religion in society and the historical tension between the spiritual non-rational and the rational makes Weber a very contemporary thinker. The relation between the information age and the new age, between commitments to rational calculation and spirituality, is very much part of current social and cultural contradictions and concerns (Wexler, 2000). One would expect a great deal of continuity from Weber's modern origins to our contemporary context. But the truth is that in social theory, particularly in education, Durkheim and Marx have been the pillars of theoretical durability, the fountainheads of traditions of social theory in education. In Weber's case, we are going to have to draw more of the educational implications from his model by ourselves. He had less to say directly about education, and his general social theoretic "heirs" are only now beginning to forcibly reassert his enduring importance (Whimster, 2000).

We can see for ourselves, and there are some broad hints in Weber's work, how the Weberian tradition is relevant to thinking about education socially. First, in addition to understanding the social process of education as being about social integration and organization or about focusing on economic production and social movements, this model underlines the importance of beliefs and ideas embodied in people's lives. Weber is a theorist of the cultural factor. Second, culture in everyday life implies for Weber an attention to the meaning that people give to their relationships with others. Ritual may be important and, obviously so are work and technology, but so too is the "subjective" understanding that we have about our social relations. We interact with each other in a world of ideas that have become meaningful to us. We define what we are doing. We don't just behave. We act and give meaning to our behavior. The deep social problem that Weber was addressing was the loss of meaning in society and its replacement with rules of procedure. His theory of social process, appropriately, is a theory of social action, of people interchanging meanings as they behave with each other.

Third, there is conflict in Weber's model. The tension and conflict for Durkheim is between too much individualism and the necessarily shared ritual togetherness of collective life. For Marx, as we have seen, there is a theoretical tension between the power of socioeconomic structures to perpetuate or "reproduce" themselves and the strength of people to consciously grasp social conditions that they share with others and to join with each other in movements of collective action and change. In practice, in Marx's model there is fundamental conflict between social groups, based in what we have called the social problems of alienation and exploitation that eventuates in class conflict.

The conflict for Weber is ultimately between two cultures. There is the triumphant culture of bureaucratic expertise and specialization, the culture of rules, procedures, and rationalization. And, there is the religious culture, which preceded and unintentionally "gave birth" to the modern culture of rationality. The historical core of the religious culture is in magic and spirituality, which appears to be historically over and done with. Not so fast. Now and again, this magical spirit, which Weber calls "charisma," breaks out again and returns—sometimes with the appearance of overwhelmingly forceful leaders, and sometimes, quietly, in the inner personal lives of people, away from the public social sphere. As we shall see, Weber had some hints to offer about what this conflict might mean for education.

The implication for us is that the durability of the Weberian tradition has to be uncovered and amplified in:

- the role of historic, particularly religious, ideas in forming culture
- the enactment of culture by the way that people give meaning to their everyday interactions
- the conflict between the cultural principles of rationality and charisma
- how these cultural dynamics play themselves out in the social process of education.

Durable Models: Continuity and Examples

While we will have more work to do in spelling out how the third model, the cultural or Weberian model, has worked out over time and in education, the continuities and examples of the first two models are more evident. There is work in Education that is known as Durkheimian or Functionalist as well as work that is called Marxist or Critical. It is possible to show the continuities with the founding creators of the models, the "giants," and to also reveal how each model is expressed in examples of empirical research in Education.

I think that the most important and ultimately useful thing is to grasp the basic concepts and intent of each model and to internalize them. If we focus on the theoretical basics, then we will have our own analytical tools, our ways of making sense of education socially. It is up to us, even as beginners, to choose, to criticize, to modify, and to apply what has been bequeathed to us by the traditions of social theory. I hope that we can show that when we work with these basic ideas, we can think about Education in a different way—which by putting it into the social process is already a critical dissent from the taken-for-granted patterns of thinking about education as somehow outside of social, economic, and cultural aspects of society. We should begin with the Durkheimian tradition, since he was the founder of mainstream sociology and the first academic, theoretical sociologist of education.

Glossary

Alienation—Marx's term for the loss of one's creative power and control over work and the products of work, a loss that results from the particular way that work is organized in capitalism.

Bureaucracy—Weber's term for a particular type of social organization where rational calculation and set rules prevail and where the goal is to maximize efficiency. Here, social action is organized in terms of rational and legal rules, rather than either tradition or charisma.

Charisma—Weber's terms, taken from Christian theology, meaning "grace." Weber uses it to refer to the extraordinary power and magnetism of historical individuals that leads people to willingly obey them. Charisma begins in magical power and stands opposed to rationality and bureaucracy.

Class—In Marx's theory, the position of people in relation to their ownership of the means of production, of who controls labor and its fruits. In capitalist societies, there are two main and opposing classes: the owners (who are the capitalist class) and the proletariat (who are workers).

Classical Sociology—Ordinarily refers to the most well-known European sociologists of the late nineteenth and early twentieth century who influenced the basic concepts, theories, and questions of later sociologists, including modern American sociologists.

Context—A shorthand way of talking about the array and constellation of social factors and forces in any situation. In our discussion, context influences knowledge, and being aware of that is referred to as reflexivity.

Enlightenment—Indicates the leading social, intellectual movement of the eighteenth century, where the scientific path of knowledge, as developed particularly by Newton becomes the general cultural ideal. In that sense, Enlightenment can be thought of as the intellectual core of modernity. Its central commitment is to reason, understood according to the natural science model. This commitment implies also that reason—and not faith, belief, and emotion—provides the direction and means toward greater human freedom and self-realization in society.

Exploitation—Marx's term for the result of the work process in which the value or wealth that the proletariat creates is returned to them only partially. Most of the wealth that their work creates is taken by the capitalist class.

Habitus—Weber's way of describing the intersection of culture and psychology. Character types, like the self-denying or ascetic Protestant, are an example of how a culture comes to work in the everyday life of people. Bourdieu later expanded this idea, writing about dispositions and about unspoken internalized rules for action that come from the context.

Ideology—Marx's term, taken from the history of French revolutionary thought, to describe how social class position and interests shape and distort thinking and ideas.

Integration—Durkheim's term to describe how society holds together. When there is a lack of shared symbols, social coordination, and a sense of common belonging, people suffer from a lack of moral regulation. "Anomie" is the unhappy result of a lack of social integration.

Model—A very general term for sets of concepts that fit together to describe and explain phenomena. In our use, classical sociology is the source of different social models, or systems of explanation.

Problematic—Refers to the package of questions asked regarding both social problems of the context and the concepts that comprise the models of explanation.

Production—Marx's term for the social organization of work or "labour." This organization of work changes historically and shapes many other aspects of society.

Reproduction—As a general term, refers to replication. While in early Marxist theory the emphasis is on the replication of workers and their life conditions, later it comes to mean the way that culture serves to replicate and continue the existing structure of society.

Romanticism—An intellectual, social movement of the late eighteenth and early nineteenth century expressed in philosophy and literature, especially poetry. Key ideas of this movement include the importance of inner experience, imagination, and creativity. Often considered a countermovement to Enlightenment, Romantic thinkers are vitalistic rather than analytic, oriented to the joy of life and the possibilities of an ongoing renewal of human energy and the reintegration of humanity and society into a dynamic wholeness.

CHAPTER TWO

Durkheimian Social Theory in Education

Sociologism

Sociologism

A not-always favorable description, often ascribed to the Durkheimian tradition, meaning an overemphasis on social explanation. A reaction to "psychologism" and its focus solely on individuals, sociologism points to an excessive reliance of the collective and social structural to explain people's actions in society.

Durkheim arrives at his own theoretical position by working from a variety of traditions (Nisbet, 1965). He begins from the methodological starting point that sociology is an independent science of society and not one reducible to psychological explanations. Society is a real. There are social facts "out there," and we can study them empirically and systematically. His own empirical exemplary study, a landmark of mainstream sociology, "Suicide" (Durkheim, 1951) demonstrates this methodology. He explains a phenomenon that is not only usually explained psychologically but is indeed also one of the most personal, subjective, internal behaviors: suicide. He explains by showing correlation or correspondence between suicide rates and social, rather than individual, characteristics. Group membership type and the extent of both social ties and social rules affect the likelihood of suicide. Those groups that are most integrated, that is, having a clear sense of membership, and those situations that are optimally regulative of individual behavior have the lowest rates of suicide.

This quintessentially individual behavior is shown to vary with social categories. The scientific aspiration to predict behavior

is actualized by showing the differential likelihood or rates of suicide as aspects of social structures and processes. Underlying the typology of social explanations of suicide that Durkheim develops is his theoretical commitment: society is an order of moral regulation. Without the right amount of adherence to shared and binding social rules (there can also be too much group binding and too much shared moral regulation), there is broad-scale, individual suffering. The condition of society affects the condition of the individual. What is most salient about society is the extent and effectiveness of its integration. Failed integration—that is, inadequate sharing of moral rules that regulate behavior—leads to social disorder and too much individualism. Suicide rates vary with the degree of social disorder or "**anomie**," and excessive individualism or "egoism." People need an integrated society of cohesive groups and effective social rules in order to insure their likelihood of survival. Social facts are of decisive importance and only the new science of sociology can effectively marshal them.

This empirical methodological assertion of a very strong, exclusively sociological view, that might be called "sociologism," is one aspect of Durkheim's emphasis on the social. In his analysis of the evolution of societal institutions (Bellah, 1973), he again wants to show that too much individualism and not enough of sociality creates social pathologies and havoc. In his evolutionary model, Durkheim repeatedly asks the question of integration. What holds societies together? What is the basis of social **solidarity**?

Anomie

Lack of a shared moral code. It is the absence of social integration that leads to social pathologies, including higher rates of suicide, in people who suffer from a lack of moral regulation.

Solidarity

The social problematic that we discussed, the worry about a poor balance between the individual and the collective, informs Durkheim's theorizing. Earlier, simpler societies held together based on resemblances or similarities among people; this insured their integration. As societal and institutional specialization increases and the division of social labor becomes more complex, largely due to demographic growth and population density, the problems of moral order, stability and equilibrium, and solidarity becomes more pressing. The complementarity of the different parts, institutions, or "organs" of society is not enough to hold them together against the centripetal power of complexities and differences. Even contracts among people do not create strong

Solidarity

Durkheim's focal term for the ways that society is integrated. His early study of the structure and function of society analyzed two different types of solidarity, one based on similarity and one based on difference. Most interpreters agree that ultimately Durkheim relies on a solidarity of similarity or shared morality and collective representations to keep society together and to prevent the social illness of anomie.

enough social ties. As Durkheim puts it (Bellah, 1973; 101), agreements between individuals or "contracts" are possible only because there are "pre-established rules." A newer, more complex solidarity based on complementary differences, a solidarity that Durkheim called "organic," is by itself not sufficient to replace the earlier form of a "mechanical" solidarity based on similarity. We need the "likeness of consciences," people sharing a common morality that binds them together and so integrates society.

"Anomie," the lack of a shared moral code is the source of social pathology and individual suffering. Durkheim is a pioneering theorist of the social, because he reverses the causal order of relation between the individual and the society. Individuals do not create societies: societies create individuals. Once created, individuals become more numerous, and simple forms of social integration based on similarity are insufficient to maintain societal stability through moral solidarity. But, in the long run, complementarity based on complexity does not work either. We need a common "moral code," which itself is the product of social life.

Durkheim saw in "occupational groups" the possibility of new ways of integrating society. He wrote about the almost religious, modern belief in the individual as a possible basis for organizing new forms of common social commitment. Ultimately, he saw two bases of social integration. One, education would create a shared commitment to a common moral code that is necessary for social integration. That is why education is importantly "moral education." Two, and even more basically, religious rituals create the sort of social energy and shared morality in a way that bring people together around common symbols and constantly recreate the social.

Religion

Durkheim's last major book, which he thought had been neglected and indeed was not ordinarily taught as his most important contribution, is about religion as the re-creative source of social solidarity. In *The Elementary Forms of Religious Life*, Durkheim writes the following (1995; 327):

> Religious forces are in fact only transfigured collective forces, that is moral forces; they are made of ideas and feelings that the spectacle of society awakens in us.

It is in religious ritual practices that "collective forces," the antidote to anomie and the disintegration of society because of inadequate solidarities, are made manifest and intensified. Shared ideas of morality—the regulative **codes** that prevent social chaos and individual suffering because of not enough regulation and too much individualism (anomie and egoism)—may be pedagogically transmitted and internalized in schools. But, the most powerful educator is the collective force of group life itself. That is where the moral code is created. As Durkheim writes (1995; 349):

> In actuality, it is in group life that these representations are formed, and group life is by nature intermittent…They achieve their greatest intensity when the individuals are assembled in direct relations with one another, at the moment when everyone communes in the same idea or emotion. Once the assembly is dissolved and each person has returned to his own existence, those representations lose more and more of their original energy.

The solution to the ongoing dissolution of socially integrative common ideas—or "**collective representations**," as Durkheim calls them—is repetitive assemblies of sociality (1995; 350):

> The only way to renew the collective representations that refer to sacred beings is to plunge them again into the very source of religious life; assembled groups.

The social is the basis of the individual. The social is under constant threat of disintegration, of the loss of solidarity. The core of solidarity is a shared moral code. The best way to create the moral code, although it may be transmitted as an educational program, is for individuals to commune with each other in ritualized assemblies focused on sacred symbols that are in fact symbols of the group itself. In their ritual communion, they generate emotional energy that is attached to representations or symbols. This shared symbolic attachment is both internalized or socialized (education) and recreated and actively regenerated (religion). "Collective consciousness is the highest form of psychic life" (1995; 445). I think we can see now why Durkheim is the social theorist of the social. We are made and remade as persons, and the organization of our common life is possible only though intense forms of sociality. The social is the source of our energy and motivation (Collins, 2004) and of our collective identity.

Code

Structure or key of organized meaning. Structuralists, such as Bernstein, are interested in the relation between social structure and language, which is a symbolic code.

Collective Representations

Durkheim's concept that is especially prominent in his last major work on sociology of religion. Shared rituals in collective assemblies lead people to have shared ideas, both about how the world works and about moral standards.

Durkheimianism in Education

Functionalism

Functionalism

A major school of American sociology, identified with the work of Parsons and his students. The Functionalist models begin, however, in much older images that societies work like human organisms; they have structures and functions. Functionalism emphasizes the systematic organization of social processes that contribute to the maintenance of the structure of society.

Talcott Parsons was the most famous and influential American academic sociologist for many years. Arguably, in his first major book, in the 1930s, *The Structure of Social Action*, he brought the classical tradition of European sociology to the attention of Americans. It is true that Marx receives short shrift in this large synthetic work in social theory and also that Parsons seems to favor Weber and to place himself in the Weberian tradition by virtue of an emphasis on meaningful social action, which, as we know, was a main line in Weber's sociology.

Yet, I would suggest that Parsons is the definitive American Durkheimian sociologist and that his theories systematized several of Durkheim's major directions and modified them within the context of the American culture of his own times. At least two of Durkheim's interrelated themes become central in Parsons' Functionalist theory of society (Parsons, 1951). One is that society should be considered in itself, at its own level, and not as the aggregation of separate individuals. This is what we called Durkheim's "sociologism." Durkheim was in critical dialogue with Spencer's work, which he saw as aggregating individuals to make society. But as we now know, that is not Durkheim's social (Bellah, 1973; 132):

> It is not necessary, then, with Spencer, to present social life as a simple resultant of individual natures since, on the contrary, it is rather the latter which comes from the former. Social facts are not the simple development of psychic facts, but the second are in large part only the prolongation of the first in the interior of consciences...it is the social organization of the relations of kinship which has determined the respective sentiments of parents and children. They would have been completely different if the social structure had been different...it is the nature of the group which along can explain them.

Parsons, over a long productive course of work (Parsons, 1966), takes the Durkheim sociologism and describes it not simply as a group or collectivity, but as a social "system" (for critiques of Parsons, see Wrong, 1956 and Gouldner, 1970). One of the main characteristics of a system is not only that the parts fit together, but also that in an organic, living system, including a society or a social system, there is a tendency for the system to

maintain itself, to keep going in its environment. This equilibrium in relation to the environment is not, however, automatic and has to be attained by structured social processes. The structures or institutions of society "function," reminiscent of structures in living organisms, to enable the maintenance of the system.

As Devereux (1961) writes in his thorough review of the key theoretical elements of Parsons' extensive body of sociological work (1960; 33): "The problem of order, integration and equilibrium have always played a central role in Parsons' thinking." Societies have their own lives, as it were, and there are certain needs or "functional prerequisites" (Levy, 1959) that every society must meet in order to maintain or reproduce itself. Parsons had his own schema of these needs or functional problems. He saw all social systems, from small groups to entire societies, as grappling with organized, socially patterned ways of meeting these system needs. Central among these functional problems, in addition to the technical, practical problems of adapting to its environment, are the more internal problems of attaining order and stability. This is Durkheim's social worry over anomie and his focus on social integration—on accomplishing social solidarity and cohesion as the bases of social life.

Parsons continues Durkheim's model of society, even while addressing the Weberian ideal of meaningful social action, in the way in which the problem of integration or order is solved. As with Durkheim, it is ultimately shared ideas, representations, and moral codes that are a defining and necessary characteristic of orderly social life. Parsons' version of Durkheim's moral code includes shared patterned values and their internalization. He follows Durkheim in other ways, although very much in the different context of mid-twentieth-century American society rather than in fin-de-siècle, turn of the nineteenth century, France. He recognizes the importance of individualism. To him, this means the value of "achievement."

In the value choices that he postulates, Parsons shows how much of the main tendency of shared values is participation in the culture of modernity. These value choices are built into social roles, which are the building blocks of institutions. Being achievement oriented, unemotional, specialized, and impersonal—the culture that Weber criticized—expresses the shared values that make modern society possible.

These values are learned and reinforced in a variety of social institutions. Parsons, having the benefit of Freud's influence, gives family the importance that Durkheim gave to religion. The family is the locus of the creation of the moral code. Public reinforcement of the achievement-individualist aspects occurs when the child leaves the family for the school. Parsons sees education in terms of its contribution to societal maintenance. Schooling plays a central role in the solution of functional problems. Their solution leads to equilibrium and social continuity, or what we would now call social "reproduction."

The social works at every level, from small groups, through organizations and societal institutions, to whole societies. Parsons shows that the school classroom too can be analyzed "as a social system" (1959). He asks what and how classroom life contributes to social integration or social order. The answer is that the school in society specializes both in social sorting, which Parsons calls "allocation," and in inculcating key shared societal values, which he calls "**socialization.**" For Functionalist social theorists, sorting into different and unequal occupational destinations is a necessary societal function (Davis and Moore, 1945). Schools help do that in a variety of organized public ways. An equally important, if not more so, social function of schooling is to represent the dominant values of "the society" and to socialize students into accepting these values as integral to their self-definitions and personalities.

Socialization

A very general sociological concept rooted in Functionalism that refers to the process in which shared societal values are internalized by individuals and become their motivation for action.

Dreeben (1968) carries Parsons' functionalist analysis of schooling further. He tries to explain exactly how schools socialize students, how students learn "norms," moral social rules, or, as Dreeben put it, "the contribution of schooling to the learning of norms." His own contribution is not only in specifying those norms, which are the norms of modern culture, in a way that Durkheim, despite his emphasis on "individualism," did not. Dreeben identifies the norms of "independence, achievement, universalism and specificity" as "what is learned in school." The school curriculum is not simply an explicit curriculum of cognitive knowledge. There is a more implicit, hidden curriculum of moral values. Moral as well as technical knowledge is taught in school. But, the way that the moral curriculum, or values, is taught is not by deliberate instruction. Durkheim's moral code and Parsons' shared values, or what he called "pattern variables,"

are learned through the way that the school is organized. They are "taught" in the social relations between teachers and students, by school practices of testing and sorting, and by the informal rules and reward systems for conformity with the dominant practices of the school institution. Schools help perform the societal functions of the allocation and socialization of youth, in their transition form private families to a public spheres of citizenship and work.

In recent years, Functionalism, as an explicit theory and as a social theory of education, has become less popular. Not that it has disappeared. Rather, there is a great deal of empirical research, especially in mainstream, academic sociology of education that asserts its independence not from Functionalism but from classical social theory in general. Nevertheless, the basic ideas of the classical tradition, notably Durkheimianism in its Functionalist version, serve as the background assumptions for research that is ostensibly removed from the classical tradition (Hallinan, 2000). Some of these affinities are acknowledged when Gamoran, Secada, and Marrett (2000) begin their summary of research on teaching and learning in "the organizational context" by writing (2000; 37): "Sociologists have a predilection for the collective. We are centrally concerned with social facts."

They go on to explain why teaching and learning can be better understood by analyzing social, organizational contextual influences than by looking at teaching and learning itself, detached from the wider society. What is especially interesting, for someone looking for the durability of Functionalism, is that one of their important societal influences is "societal norms and expectations." We appear to be far from the theoretical and critical language of classical sociology, but our concepts, even in somewhat different terms, remain linked to classical concerns—norms, expectations, moral codes, and collective representations, to use Durkheim's language.

Structuralism

Society can be studied at its own social level, and not as the summation of individuals. Like a living organism, it has needs or functions that have to be performed for survival. Integration and moral regulation are necessary social functions to which the institutions and representations of shared values and beliefs

contribute. These institutions and representations also have a certain form or structure.

For Durkheim, the problem of social integration and its failed "pathology," the social problem of "anomie," arises from changes in the structure of society (Durkheim in Bellah, 1973). Simpler societies have less specialization of functions, which he called "the division of labor." They hold together based on resemblance and similarity. The structure of societies changes as they as they become more complex due to an advancing division of labor and specialization. In simpler societies, social integration or "solidarity" based on similarity is a "mechanical solidarity." In complex societies, where the division of labor has advanced, it brings with it not only more differences, including individualism, but also new social problems, such as anomie. In the society of complexity and difference, achieving social integration is more difficult, although there is a more complex, "organic" solidarity.

This structural aspect of Durkheim, which centers on the changing forms of the division of labor and the types of solidarity, has also influenced social theorizing about education. Basil Bernstein (1973, 1996) takes up this structuralist aspect by showing how Durkheim's theory of division of labor and solidarity can be applied to language. Following the Durkheimian tradition of linking the individual and the collective by moral education, Bernstein researches and theorizes the structure of language in family and school. He openly acknowledges and admires Durkheim, giving us a clear hint of how Durkheim's work is important for his own social theory of education (1973; 474):

> Durkheim's work is a truly magnificent insight into the relationships between symbolic orders, social relationships and the structuring of experience...He raised the whole question of the relation between the classification and frames of the symbolic order and the structure of experience. In his study of the different forms of social integration he pointed to the implicit, condensed symbolic structure of mechanical solidarity and the more explicit and differentiated symbolic structures of organic solidarity.

Bernstein's interest in socialization is not like the Functionalist internalization of the content of shared values. Rather, he is interested in the nature of language, especially its structure, and how that stands between social contexts on the one hand and thinking and learning on the other. He borrows also from the

Marxist tradition by being interested in how differences in social context and the structure of language may be patterned by differences in social class position.

His main early research interest, following the quote from Durkheim, was to show how different forms of social structure create different structures of speech. Mechanical and organic solidarity are two types of social structures and we can see in different types of social interactions, first in the family and then in the school, how each has its own structure of language. As Bernstein observes (1973; 479): "Communalised roles have given way to individualised roles, condensed symbols to articulated symbols." Put in plainer language, it means that his research showed that working class families and middle class families, as examples of social contexts, had different social structures and also different forms of speech. In social groups that are structured more on the basis of similarity and, therefore, can have more implicit forms of communication with each other, one style of speech, or "code," as Bernstein calls it, develops. In other contexts, organized more on the basis of difference and implicit communication, as in the middle class family, for example, we get another linguistic code. He calls the first type a "restricted" code and the second, an "elaborated" one, indicating that this is a more differentiated language and one less tied to its context. It is more abstract and "universal," since it develops in a more fluid, individualized social context.

Schools as well as families have linguistic/speech or what Bernstein calls "symbolic codes." It is not hard to see how this analysis can lead to social criticism and political debates about differences as inequalities. What if the family has one speech code and the knowledge and pedagogy of the school is organized around a different code, which it claims to be the correct educational code?

The work of Bernstein and his colleagues and students (see Sadovnik, 1995; *British Journal of Sociology of Education*, 2002) increasingly aimed to analyze the symbolic code of schools. The later research and theory takes the theory of codes derived from Durkheim's types of solidarity and studied by Bernstein in families and applies it to the structure of knowledge and teaching in schools—curriculum and pedagogy. Unlike Functionalists—who ask about what the educational process does for other social institutions and for society as a whole, and who often study the informal, hidden curriculum—Bernstein is an example of the structuralist interest in the internal organization or structure of knowledge and its communication.

In his later work, Bernstein's "theory of codes" (1996) moves toward this more internal, structural analysis of curriculum and pedagogy. He openly criticizes "cultural reproduction" for not paying enough attention to the "internal," to the school itself. Curriculum can be analyzed according to its "classification," the boundaries or degrees of "insulation" between different types of knowledge: for example, are school subjects strongly separated or classified, or are they part of a more fluid interdisciplinarity, for example? Similarly, teaching, or "pedagogy," can be understood according to its "framing," which is the structure of control of communicating knowledge. Here too, strong boundaries will lead to one sort of pedagogy, a "visible" pedagogy, while a "weak" control or regulation of the relation between what Bernstein calls "transmitters and acquirers" is an "invisible pedagogy."

The language of the theory itself can be tricky, and many people find reading Bernstein's work difficult. Yet, I think, we do grasp the main lines of his argument, particularly if we understand it as within the Durkheimian tradition. Here we have the structural aspect of Durkheim's "sociologism," of studying society at its own level and not thinking about it as the sum of individuals. Society is its own level of reality. Like a living organism, it has functions and structures (you might ask, "Is Education the heart of society?"). Bernstein takes Durkheim's whole society or "macro" level analysis of the division of labor and forms of solidarity and brings it to smaller groups and specific institutions, such as families and schools, to a "micro" analysis. He underlines not so much the content of Durkheim's moral code as its form or structure.

Despite these differences and his own specialized vocabulary, Bernstein is asking Durkheimian questions. How can we analyze social facts? If knowledge and teaching are important social facts, then we ought to describe them precisely, even if it is difficult and if the social facts are "representations," society's shared symbolic codes. Bernstein's interest in moving from the macro to the micro level also belongs to the Durkheimian tradition. We see it among Functionalists such as Parsons, as well as

among Structuralists such as Bernstein. This linking of levels is about the original Durkheimian problem, both as a practical and as a theoretical social question. What is the relation between the individual and the collective?

The nature of the relation between them is important in Education. Whether we speak of socialization or message acquisition, or of internalization versus linguistic competence, of personality or identity, the question remains about how we become social beings. Because he posed these sorts of questions, Durkheim remains a central figure in the social theory of education. His "heirs" demonstrate not only tensions and contradictions within the tradition, but also its durability.

Interactionism

Interactionism

While it has a particular meaning in the history of American sociology, this is not the emphasis here. We are underlining the differences between Functionalism, Structuralism, and Interactionism. Here it means a more local, small-scale, or "micro" level approach, and a special emphasis on the dynamic processual aspect of social relationships.

There is a content to social facts and a structure, and also a process. Durkheim's theory is a social theory. At the heart of this theory is an interest in how the social is created and continued or reproduced. Collins (2004) interprets Durkheim's theory of integration and solidarity at the "local" level. He tries to explain how the moral, cognitive, and emotional order of society is created through social interaction. Ritual is the main path of cultural and moral order, since it generates "emotional energy." The emotional energy that is created in shared ritual interactions is the bridge between the social and the individual. Collins is interested in starting from the ground up, and not from global structures. He calls this "microsociology" (Collins, 2004; 3): "A theory of interaction ritual is the key to microsociology." The religious rituals that Durkheim described become the model for an interaction interpretation, as Collins combines Goffman's theory of everyday social life with Durkheim's theory of social solidarity and societal integration. The global, large-scale or "macro" social is the result of the "micro" of social interaction. Ritual is the key element in social interaction. It results in Durkheim's centerpiece: how to combat "anomie" and create solidarity (Collins, 2004; 7) "ritual is a mechanism of mutually focused emotion and attention producing a momentarily share reality, which thereby generates solidarity and symbols of group membership."

Here is a Durkheimian interactionism that provides the micro elements or building blocks of a society that is neither

Functionalist of Structuralist. Lomsky-Feder (2004) offers an ethnographic account of school life in Israel. She too starts from a Durkheimian interest in ritual but then goes on to show how school ceremonies do not just produce social order. In a more complex way, the school ceremonies or collective rituals that she analyzes show how different groups (2004; 292) "negotiate over or even contest the writing of the national past." She is referring here to school memorial ceremonies that do not just strengthen solidarity and integration. Rather, they become a field for reinterpreting shared, national collective memories. The ceremony is an active interaction. As she writes (2004; 302) "School memorial ceremonies constitute a diversified interpretive field, which includes canonic characteristics and elements of innovation and resistance." The "canon" is the shared moral and cognitive social order. In performing ceremonies, in interacting with each other, participants rewrite them, do them differently, and even challenge shared values and memories. Here, the Durkheimian interest in ritual becomes not only interactive but also conflictual and part of a process of historic change.

Glossary

Anomie—Lack of a shared moral code. It is the absence of social integration that leads to social pathologies, including higher rates of suicide, in people who suffer from a lack of moral regulation.

Code—Structure or key of organized meaning. Structuralists, such as Bernstein, are interested in the relation between social structure and language, which is a symbolic code.

Collective Representation—Durkheim's concept that is especially prominent in his last major work on sociology of religion. Shared rituals in collective assemblies lead people to have shared ideas, both about how the world works and about moral standards.

Functionalism—A major school of American sociology, identified with the work of Parsons and his students. The Functionalist models begin, however, in much older images that societies work like human organisms; they have structures and functions. Functionalism emphasizes the systematic organization of social processes that contribute to the maintenance of the structure of society.

Interactionism—While it has a particular meaning in the history of American sociology, this is not the emphasis here.

We are underlining the differences between Functionalism, Structuralism, and Interactionism. Here it means a more local, small-scale, or "micro" level approach, and a special emphasis on the dynamic processual aspect of social relationships.

Socialization—A very general sociological concept rooted in Functionalism that refers to the process in which shared societal values are internalized by individuals and become their motivation for action.

Sociologism—A not-always favorable description, often ascribed to the Durkheimian tradition, meaning an overemphasis on social explanation. A reaction to "psychologism" and its focus solely on individuals, sociologism points to an excessive reliance of the collective and social structural to explain people's actions in society.

Solidarity—Durkheim's focal term for the ways that society is integrated. His early study of the structure and function of society analyzed two different types of solidarity, one based on similarity and one based on difference. Most interpreters agree that ultimately Durkheim relies on a solidarity of similarity or shared morality and collective representations to keep society together and to prevent the social illness of anomie.

CHAPTER THREE

Marxist Social Theory in Education

While Marxism, as a social theory and as a social movement, has a history of more than a century and a half, it is a relative newcomer to social theory in Education. We can speculate on the reasons for this and our speculations will take us back to the beginning of our study: social theory develops in a historical context. Without trying to prove exactly why and how Marxism was excluded from academic discourse, notably in the United States, the fact of the matter is that only with the rise of the so-called "New Left" in the 1960s did Marx's theory of society begin to become more widely known outside of its political uses in what were once "communist" countries.

Within Education, the rediscovery and the analytical uses of Marxism are even more recent and narrower in scope. The introduction of Marxist social theory to Education followed the wider reinterpretation of Marx in Europe and then in the American cultural revolution of the 1960s. A decade later, the Marxist influence became prominent first in England and then only later in the United States, where it was variously termed "radical," "critical," "neo-Marxist," or, more lastingly, "the new sociology of education" (Wexler, 2007a). Here too, we can see how much

social theory may be context-bound and historically limited. After a period of about twenty-five years of broad influence on social thinking about education, Marxism receded, apparently replaced by newer "postmodern" theories of education (Wexler, 2007a).

Our view is different. Social theory is historical and contextual. But, it is also trans-contextual. It has meaning and explanatory power beyond the cultural contexts that favor and disseminate one particular theory over another. We are interested in powerful and elegant social models, sets of concepts that can help explain education as a social process. Marxist theory offers one of the most coherent, systematic theories of society and includes basic concepts that we continue to think are important in interpreting education socially. Perhaps, under various theoretical umbrellas, such as "critical pedagogy" (Kincheloe, 2004; Kincheloe and McLaren, 2007), there is now a renaissance not only of classical sociology in general, but of Marxism in particular (McCarthy, 2003; McLennan, 2000). Whether we are going to see a "new" "new sociology of education" or not I cannot foretell. But, I do think that Marx's theory of society has shaped our general models of social explanation, and that it has a tradition, although still a brief one, as a foundational pillar of social theories in Education.

Marx's Words

We don't have to be cynical about interpretation. It is true that the same text can be read differently, by different people, at different times, and in different places. The interpretive or "hermeneutic" approach to the meaning of texts and of even trying to fathom the author's real intention is important and helps broaden our understanding of the different facets and complexity of theories. With Marx, the interpretive multiplicity is compounded by the overtly political nature of his work and of its very wide international reception over the course of many, many decades.

Nevertheless, in the face of such a dauntingly large literature of interpreting Marx, of almost a "Marxology," I do think that we can take from Marx's texts some very basic and clear understandings of how to analyze society. By trying to understand Marx

in his own words, we could be closer to our goal of developing models as tools to be used in our own social analyses of education. If we want to read Marx as a social theorist, then we are going to see what the implications for this particular tradition of theory are for a social understanding of education.

Just as Durkheim reacted against psychological, individualist explanations in a way that spurred him to develop a science of society, of social facts, Marx is reacting against a long history of German philosophy that explained historical development as the result of ideas, spirit, and mind. Marx is in reaction against these more mental explanations of social life and he wants to bring social understanding down to earth, to everyday practical activities. "I was led," he writes, "by my studies to the conclusion that legal relations as well as forms of the State could neither be understood by themselves nor explained by the so-called general progress of the human mind, but that they are rooted in the material conditions of human life" (in Bottomore and Rubel, 1956; 51). Marx continues that he is interested in "the real foundation." What is the real foundation of the historical mind, legal relations, the state, and social consciousness? I think that there is no interpretive improvement that can be made on Marx's words themselves (p. 51):

> The **mode of production** of material life determines the general character of the social, political and spiritual processes of life. It is not the consciousness of men that determines their being, but on the contrary, their social being determines their consciousness.

People like to say that Marx "turned on its head" German idealist philosophy. Maybe so. What is important for us, however, is that in trying to do that he offers a rich and comprehensive model of how society works.

We said at the outset that compared to Durkheim's social approach, Marx's is economic. Marx tells us exactly what he means by this economic approach to social life (p. 53):

> Men can be distinguished from animals by consciousness, by religion, or by anything one likes. They themselves begin to distinguish themselves from animals as soon as they begin to produce...In producing their means of subsistence men indirectly produce their actual material life.

Mode of Production

Marx uses the term to refer to the overall social and economic organization of the work process in which people produce what they need to live ("use") as well as to what is produced for the marketplace and profit ("exchange"). The mode of production includes the forces of production—especially technology and the social processes closest to it; and the social relations of production, which includes not only property ownership, but also most other political and social arrangements. One of Marx's hypotheses is that the forces of production change faster than the social relations of production. This conflict, within the structure, basically between technology and property relations, is what leads classes to act and to cause fundamental revolutionary social changes.

The "economic" character of Marx's social theory is that he gives a clear priority to the economic, which means production, working, and making:

> As individuals express their life, so they are. What they are, therefore, coincides with their production, with what they produce and how they produce it. What individuals are therefore, depends on the material conditions of their production.

There are different modes of production, including ancient and feudal, and for the modern era, "bourgeois" or capitalist production. These modes of production include both the technology used and the way that work is organized in the process of producing. These are the forces of production. These productive forces or processes are nested in ever-widening aspects of society, in the social relations of production. Here, relations of ownership and control are central and are the bases of the division of society into antagonistic groups or "classes." In the bourgeois or capitalist mode of production, for example, control of the productive process belongs to the capitalist class. The working class, the proletariat, is the majority and is the ultimate source of wealth in society.

The antagonism of classes is based then not only on positions of relative control or powerlessness in the process of production, but also on the appropriation of wealth from the producers by the owners of the means of production. Marx's economic theory is that social wealth is created by labor. In capitalist societies, the class of workers, who were uprooted from their agricultural way of life through which they sustained themselves in the feudal mode of production, sells this value possession, labor, in order to live. They are remunerated for their work, but the value of their remuneration is less than the value of what they produce. They work more labor time than would be necessary to just pay them enough for sustenance. The value of the additional labor time that they work is, however, not returned to them but goes instead to the owners, the capitalist class. This is the technical meaning of "exploitation." What is exploited is that difference of additional labor—the "surplus value" that is the source of profit.

This economic aspect of Marx's social theory is central. Production, labor, and exploitation are meant specifically. Class and class conflict have an economic basis. But, Marx wants to go beyond the economic to the social, in a way reminiscent of the how Durkheim wants to go beyond religion to all aspects of social life. As we move outward from the economic in Marx, we should not deny the priority that he gives to the production process, both in its broader social organization and in technology in particular. Marx writes (1956; 95):

> In acquiring new forces of production, men change their mode of production, their way of earning their living; they change all their social relations. The hand mill will give you a society with the feudal lord, the steam mill a society with the industrial capitalist.

This productive emphasis and the set of technology-based priorities are sometimes referred to as a "materialist" conception of history. Recall Marx's starting point, in opposition to mind, spirit, and ideas, as the moving force of historical change. His production-based materialism does indeed reverse the order of causality among different social factors. The mode of production is real life for Marx, and he is ever wary of ideas and beliefs, especially religious beliefs. One of his most famous phrases expresses this materialist determinism (1956; 75): "Life is not determined by consciousness, but consciousness by life."

Ideas have a part to play in social life, but they are secondary to material production. It follows also that if ideas reflect "life," which is to say material production, then people with different positions in the production process will have different ideas. These differences will not be neutral, tolerant differences because the most important difference—the difference of class—in social position is antagonistic or conflictual. Classes have different ideas and because they are in conflict, ideas enter into their economically based conflict. "Consciousness" or ideas is not above real life for Marx. It is part of the social process, which is a production- and class-organized social process. This is one basis of Marx's understanding of ideas as not neutral. On the contrary, they are part of the conflicts over power, grounded in economic antagonism (1956; 78):

> The ideas of the ruling class are, in every age, the ruling ideas, i.e. the class which is the dominant material force in society is at the same time the dominant intellectual force.

In the tradition of Marxist theory, when we read social theory in education about "ideology" and how ideas are political, including

educational ideas, and about curricula that is presented without awareness of its social context and social implication, we can hear Marx's words about consciousness, ideas, and the ruling class. Despite all their differences, Marx shares with Durkheim the view that it is "the social" that shapes the individual. Society is not the sum of individual psychologies. In Marx's words (1956; 68): "The real nature of man is the totality of social relations." For Durkheim, however, the social is ritual assembly. For Marx, it is social production. These are keys to remembering the deep differences that divide the models of social theory in education.

Marx in a Jiffy

There is one more aspect of Marx that is central to this tradition of social theory. That is the term "alienation." Although we sometimes use the term generally to mean a subjective feeling of being disconnected, for Marx it has a very specific objective and, not surprisingly, an economic social origin and meaning. Like "exploitation," "alienation" is not only an analytical term, but also a critical one. It points to what is wrong, according to Marx, with the capitalist society, and it reminds us how much critical and analytical terms are bound up with each other. Here is how Marx prefaces his discussion of alienation (1956; 169, 170): "However, alienation shows itself not merely in the result, but also in the process, of production, within productive activity itself."

Since the word has had so many different uses, it is worthwhile to read Marx's words:

> In what does this alienation of labour consist? First the work is external to the worker, that it is not a part of his nature, that consequently he does not fulfill himself in his work but denies himself, has a feeling of misery, not of well-being, does not develop freely a physical and mental energy, but is physically exhausted and mentally debased. The worker therefore feels himself at home only during his leisure, whereas at work he feels homeless. His work is not voluntary, but forced labour…
>
> The more the worker expends himself in work, the more powerful becomes the world of objects which he creates in face of himself and the poorer he himself become in his inner life, the less he belongs to himself.

Marx compares alienation to religion. He sees religion as the model of disempowerment that occurs in the capitalist labor

process. The person's power is attributed to someone or something else, something beyond themselves, which becomes wrongly elevated in importance and idealized, instead of we, ourselves, who are the source of those virtues. That is what happens in the capitalist work process.

The products of our labor—which are objects that are made for the market rather than our own use, for sale- or exchange-value rather than use-value—are called "**commodities**." In a society of commodity production, we forget that the value of the product comes from our labor that is embodied in it. Instead, we falsely attribute our creative power to the commodity. In this way, we make a "fetish" of the commodity. This "fetishism of commodities" and the commodifying of all of our social relations, even beyond the work place, is a theme that recurs in the tradition of Marxist theory. We can already begin to think about education and about teaching and learning in relation to production, about ideas and class and about alienation and commodifying the social process of education in society.

One of the main differences that we will see among Marxist social theorists is how much they emphasize the other side of Marx's apparent contradiction that "men make their own history, but they do not make it just as they please." Marx's theory, indeed, like Durkheim's (with vastly different social content), is a structural and functional social theory. It is about how the social is structured beyond the sum of the individuals in an organized and collective history of production processes that are complex and internally contradictory. The internal contradiction, for example, between changing technology and the social relations of production in which it is embedded is a driving force in the historical change of societies. It has an aura of automatic inevitability about it. Society is a dynamic structure. But, where are the people? This "people" side of society emerges alongside the structuralist to explain change.

While it may be true that changing technologies make older ways of organizing social life untenable—think of the social effects of the Internet (Castells, 1997)—it is also true that people act not only within social structures but also against them; they sometimes act together, collectively in social movements. Marx recognizes this aspect too in a theory of revolution that depends on class collective actions. Structural dynamics may not be enough for radical change. People can, despite all of Marx's

Commodity

A key concept for Marx, indicating products that are made for sale, rather than for use by its producers or workers. Commodity fetishism means that people who make the products and certainly those who consume them lose sight that the products embody the efforts, the work of the producers. Ultimately, we attribute all power to the commodity and none to the producer. Commodification means that not only economic production of things, but also all other aspects of social life, such as friendship, family, and learning, take on the form of the commodity.

reservations about the power of ideas and the secondary nature of consciousness, become socially conscious. They can become aware of their social class position and understand how the wider social structure functions. With this awareness, or "class consciousness," they can recognize their affinity with others and begin to communicate, share common views, and organize collective action. They create new social movements that change society.

In structure and movement, we have two faces of Marxist theory. They appear in Marxist social theory of education—in concepts of correspondence, resistance, reproduction, ideology, class, and social movement. As with Durkheimian theory, there isn't just one type of Marxist social theory, particularly on Education.

Critical Theory

Domination

A term used by the Frankfort School of Critical Theory to indicate that submission to the will of others is not just based on forceful power. Deep power is reinforced by belief or culture and psychology. In Critical Theory, the working class remains dominated, accepting its condition in part because of the effectiveness of the power of mass culture. Domination is similar to Weber's concept of "authority," where people obey because they believe that it is right. The reasons for their belief are different and include the traditional, the rational, and the charismatic.

If society is divided into two classes, the exploited and the exploiters, why do the exploited not revolt more regularly and overthrow their oppressors? The answer to this question is at the heart of the Frankfurt School's "critical theory" of society (Horkheimer 1972a, 1972b). As they put it: "Why have the oppressed borne the yoke so long?" It is because elites rule not simply by virtue of their economic position and political power. They rule by **"domination,"** by obtaining the acquiescence and agreement of the less powerful by cultural and psychological means. Marx's economic theory of social production is taken as an essential but incomplete starting point and expanded to include Freudian psychology as well as a reinterpretation of the role of knowledge and culture in society. It is a "critical" fusion, since modern capitalist society is seen as not only unequal but also destructive of the development of human possibility and potential. In their terms, critical theory begins with an "existential judgment" about what kind of society we are living in.

The "Enlightenment" view is that knowledge, particularly scientific knowledge and also art and high culture, will liberate us and make us freer and happier. Science and culture are ordinarily considered progressive and positive. The Frankfurt School idea is that knowledge, despite its emancipatory promise, is part and parcel of an overall society that builds around the economic process a total way of life that limits and restricts human freedom and possibility. There are two sides to knowledge, a double-edged sword, a "dialectic of Enlightenment."

Family life, advertising, movies, and radio (they worked in Germany and the United States, from the 1920s to the 1960s) are deceptive. They promise us something different than the monotonous, unequal, and unsatisfying world of work, but instead, they return to us the same "iron system" of capitalism. In fact, they reinforce capitalism by offering a false freedom, one that diverts our attention, distracts us, binds us to habitual inequality, and blocks the development of our awareness and understanding of the social relations of production and work. Critical theory goes beyond production, but only to show how the system of production is constantly reinforced by the way that daily life is organized.

The prevailing knowledge, the science of "facts," leads us to take the social world as taken-for-granted and given, unchangeable and ahistorical. It creates a resigned but sometimes "happy" acceptance of the status quo, while closing the doors to alternative ways of thinking and being. This work of shoring up the "factual mentality" takes place in the patriarchal family, which teaches that unequal authority and submission and obedience are somehow "natural" and not specific to a particular historical time and mode of production. Similarly the "culture industry" of Hollywood casts a "spell of the taken for granted" in its representations of what life is and should be, like.

The work of critical theory is to unmask the "natural" and to show how it is social. To show how power works not only by brute force, but also by the domination of internalized psychologies of obedience and submission: to show how social "science" describes relationships among aspects of social life but does not ask about their deeper meaning and about how they are related to a wider historical structure of social production; to show that culture does not simply provide amusement but is a subtle initiation rite into a repetitive and monotonous system of social relationships; to show how sex is not simply liberating, but also pacifying and causing diversion of attention from more profoundly alternative ways of thinking and feeling.

Critical theory—beginning with the German Frankfurt School that influenced American critical social theory (Wexler, 2007a) in general and critical education and pedagogy—has provided a bridge from Marx's economic theory of the social

to a more comprehensive cultural and psychological analysis of alienation, exploitation, class conflict, and the social relations of production.

Reproduction in Society, Culture, and Education

A central theme that unites the seminal Frankfurt School critical theory of society, unlike more orthodox, economistic interpretations of Marx, with other strands of so-called Western Marxism, and ultimately, Education, is the interest in "reproduction."

Economic social organization—that is, the work or labor process and the unequal positions within it—requires constant renewal to insure the continuity of the structure. This renewal occurs by creating the environment not only for production, but also for the reproduction of labor power, the workers themselves, and of the structure within which they function. Psychological and cultural factors make possible the continuity of this capitalist structure and are also a key to understanding possible forms of social action and movement that might change it. The processes by which the structure is continued are generally described under the rubric of "reproduction."

There are different terms and views of what is important in this broad social, cultural, and psychological set of processes that work to continue the status quo. We might even say that the emphasis on reproduction within the broadly Marxist tradition of social theory parallels the difference between structuralism and functionalism among the Durkheimian models. Reproduction processes specify how the structured system is able to be maintained and continued, how it "works." It might be thought of as a Marxist Functionalism. As in Durkheimian Functionalism, there are different varieties, examples, and terms that reflect this interest in how the socially structured process of production is continued, replicated, or reproduced.

The most famous is "ideology." I recall, once when I was a graduate student (about a hundred years ago!), I set out to collect and write down all the definitions of the term "ideology." It took me a very long time. If, however, we take the educational angle, we can see how the various emphases on reproduction within Marxism alter our understanding of education. With Althusser (1971), ideology is an imaginary or distorted relation to what is

real. In fact, this is part of the long tradition of ideological interpretation of the deforming and untruthful relation between social
"reality" and ideas (Frankfurt School, 1972c; 183). Ideology is a
lie or error induced by the influence of social interests on ideas.
It is not socially neutral. Althusser's theory of ideology suggests
the "state apparatuses," importantly including education, play
the role of inculcating ideology by creating types of people—
"interpellating the subject," he calls it—that facilitate the reproduction needed to maintain the capitalist system of production.
This institutional reproductive work that was once done especially
in religion is now increasingly accomplished by education. Schools
are not free-floating institutions. They are part of the "State apparatus," representatives of the dominant system.

Bourdieu

Within the French school of critical theory, although
Bourdieu (1990) was very much a critic of Althusser for being
too structuralist, he is also deeply interested in reproduction, particularly in his early work (for a collection reviewing Bourdieu's
work, see the *British Journal of Sociology of Education,* September,
2004). Social reproduction of the organization of society works
through cultural reproduction. Schools, and indeed, museums
and bookshops/libraries, and other cultural institutions are
places where, as he puts it, the "power and privilege" of socially
unequal classes are "transmitted." School practice or pedagogy
is an act of "symbolic violence." The reason that it is symbolic
violence is that it is, to translate it into our terms, ideological in
the traditional sense of lies and distortion.

The lie of cultural reproduction in education is not simply
that by reproducing culture, social reproduction or the maintenance of the social structures of inequality is accomplished.
It is not only that different social groups and classes have different levels of cultural richness or "cultural capital." It is not
only that the "agents"(people) of the structure have different
"dispositions" or personal characteristic ways of acting, which
Bourdieu calls "habitus." Rather, the reproduction of unequal
cultural capital in educational settings in a way that reinforces
or reproduces the social structure is critiqued by Bourdieu as
"violent" and "concealing" very simply because it falsely presents itself as "neutral." Just as the "state apparatus" created the

subjects that it needs to function, so too does the "concealing" of cultural capital in education work in favor of social reproduction. Cultural institutions, including education conceived broadly, reward differentially on the basis of conformity to their culture. The culture of the institutions is the dominant culture. Children come from families with different levels of cultural capital and bring different levels of cultural competence to educational sites, where they are evaluated in terms of the culture of the dominant groups—which presents itself as "neutral."

Here are a few examples of the precise way that Bourdieu expresses this relation between social reproduction and cultural reproduction and the place of education within this process. What I call the "ideology" core process of the interest in reproduction is succinctly captured by Bourdieu in this way (1974; 495):

> the uneven distribution of cultural capital, all the while concealing it and, at the same time, legitimating it.

or, the same idea, a bit more complexly (496):

> this educational system masks more thoroughly than any other legitimation mechanism...the arbitrary nature of the actual demarcation of its public, thereby imposing more subtly the legitimacy of its products and its hierarchies.

and, now more directly and critically (496):

> By making social hierarchies and the reproduction of these hierarchies appear to be based upon the hierarch of "gifts," merits, or skills, in a word, by converting social hierarchies into academic hierarchies, the educational system fulfills a function of legitimation.

and, even more plainly and critically (497):

> the most culturally privileged find their way into institutions capable of reinforcing their advantage.

The job of sociology of education or, in our context, a social theory of education is (487):

> to determine the contribution made by the educational system to the reproduction of the structure of power relationships and symbolic relationships between classes, by contributing to the reproduction of the structure of the distribution of cultural capital among these classes.

We might want to point out that Bourdieu's later work moves away from the Marxist Functionalism of cultural reproduction. The dispositions or "habitus" becomes more flexible and the structures become more open and less integrated, as "fields," and the "agents" have more freedom in social action. Nevertheless, Bourdieu remains a valuable example (though he would not want to be categorized in the Marxist tradition, nor in the Durkheimian or Weberian, for that matter; 1990; 27) of how Marx's economic theory of the social is extended to include the cultural.

Critical social theories of ideology, domination, and reproduction share this wider cultural, psychological creation of social understanding on the basis of Marx's theory of production. It is interesting that for the Marxist tradition, as with the Durkheimian, both religion and education play a central role in enabling the maintenance and continuation of the social structure. Also, in both traditions, religion is seen as increasingly giving way to education as the site of reproduction and dissent from it.

Marxist Social Theory and Educational Research

Texts

In Education, Marxism itself was brought "down to earth." Early work on applying Marxist social theory to Education emphasized theory. Marxist theory was being learned and taught by Educationists (Sharp, 1980). Marx's own real world focus soon found expression among educators who applied Marxist theory to empirical research about education.

Especially in American Education, there is a long tradition of apparently atheoretical research and practice. The seeming importance in schools of practical matters and measurement alone did, of course, reflect theoretical commitments. These were the commitments to psychology, the dominant perspective. What changed with the application of Marxism to Education was that the social meaning of education became more important. Unlike an earlier social view in Education of liberal reform and the Progressive movement (Wexler, 2007a; 17) that introduced a general social view, the new wave of Marxism was more socially defined.

Its definition was critical and used the tradition of Marxist social theory to guide research. The critique of ideology in general can also be a critique of ideology in schools. With influences

from earlier works, including Bourdieu, Apple (1971) showed how to think about school curricula not as sorting devices working under the name of individual achievement, but that, as Anyon (1979) put it, "school knowledge is examined as a social product." Apple (1982) has shown how school curricula is part of the wider process of social and cultural reproduction described by Bourdieu and related it to Marx's social, the economic dimension. This economic relation between school curricula or school knowledge, which is understood not only as social but also as economic, and as part of class structure.

Educational practice—teaching and learning, school organization, and, centrally, the curriculum itself—belongs to wider social and economic processes. The content of curriculum and which curricula are more valued, "high status knowledge," as Apple calls it, are best understood by seeing how it fits with economic structures, processes, and needs. We can understand inequality in school knowledge as related to inequality in society, both economic and political inequality. Not only is knowledge stratified, reflecting structured economic differences, but also what Apple refers to, in an economic term, as the "distribution" of knowledge expresses the social reality of class society. This political and economic social reality can be seen in all aspects of curriculum, a field of practice and research that was once thought of as a purely technical or psychological question. Marxist social theory leads to research questions about the political economy of the adaptation of textbooks, of the educational policy and school reform, and, of course, of the content of school knowledge itself.

Anyon's well-known research example of this sort of research is a study of U.S. history textbooks from the vantage point of Marxist theory. As she summarizes it (1979; 379):

> This analysis of the way seventeen textbooks describe a critical period in United States and labor history demonstrates that the story told is not neutral vis-à-vis the perspective of the various groups involved. A whole range of curriculum selections favors the interests of the wealthy and powerful.

Ethnography

A style of research, originally from Anthropology, that in doing social analyses pays special attention to the people's or participants' own views and ways of life. In Education, it is sometimes called "qualitative research," to differentiate it from statistical methods of social analysis. Critical ethnography is a more specialized term that aims to signal that the theory behind the observations of "real" people in their "natural" settings is derived from Marxism and Critical Theory. Critical ethnography has interests that are not only descriptive and explanatory but also value-based and social change-oriented.

Experience and Ethnography

Apple's economic emphasis offers a bridge toward additional research in Education influenced by Marxism. One aspect of the economic, a basis of our thinking about the production process, is the centrality of labor power. Labor as the source of value in production also needs to be reproduced, and the reproduction of labor power is one of the main social "functions" of schools and of unequal labor in a class-driven capitalist society. The textual focus highlights how much of what we know, the "cognitive," is ideology. If we recall Althusser's approach to ideology that "interpellates subjects" and put that in plain language, then we are led to the idea that our personalities, character, identity, and the experiences and knowledge that make them up alongside cognition are also an important part of social production.

If schools teach ideology, they also create types of persons for labor, which is hardly "neutral" and is, in fact, alienating and exploitative as part of the very structure of society. The psychological as well as the cultural factor comes back into the educational picture. But, it does so as a social psychology—a social psychology that is integral and specific to a certain type of society. Bowles and Gintis (1976) want to explain "consciousness" and "personal behavior and development." Unlike traditional psychologists, they understand the personal socially in the context of what we have called Marx's economic social. Schools produce labor, including these personal aspects by communicating, as Parsons and Dreeben described it in a functionalist Durkheimian way, by the way the schooling is organized.

In their term, this works through the "correspondence principle." As they write (1976):

> The educational system helps integrate youth into the economic system, we believe, through a structural correspondence between its social relations and those of production.

The organization of schools affects consciousness and personal characteristics by rewarding some behaviors rather than others. There are at least two major mechanisms that they emphasize. One is that—like the unequal, hierarchical social organization of labor in the workplace—schools are organized to reward "submission to authority." In statistical analyses correlating personal characteristics and school achievement, indicated by grades, Bowles and Gintis cite studies that indicate that beyond cognitive performance, personality traits that reflect the social organization

of capitalist labor in schools as well as in the workplace best predict success and failure:

> The only significant penalized traits are precisely those which are incompatible with conformity to the hierarchical division of labor—creativity, independence, and aggressivity. On the other hand, all the personality traits which we would expect to be rewarded are, and significantly so.

They go on to show that the "submission to authority" trait demanded by an alienated organization of labor—in terms of our vocabulary of Marxist social theory—leads to success. Their conclusion is that "at least from this sample, the personality traits rewarded in schools seem to be rather similar to those indicative of good job performance in the capitalist economy."

The reproduction of the sort of workers that an exploitative—to again use a classic Marxist term—process of production requires means hierarchy, dominance, and submission in the school. Bowles and Gintis recognize that not all levels of education are the same. There is a "correspondence," or parallel structure, between "different levels of education (that) feed workers into different levels with the occupational structure." The organization of work may be alienated and exploitative, generally. But, not all work and educational organizations are equally so. There is inequality and hierarchy among organizations, just as among individuals. The differences and hierarchies of educational organizations correspond to the differences among work organizations and to different levels of how work is organized for different employees in the same organization.

Some levels of work require clear "rule-following" for job performance. Others demand "dependability," and in still others, work is done without constant and immediate supervision. In this last case, job performance is based on the workers' internalization of the norms of the enterprise. In the first level, rule-following is at the lowest level of the organization. In the second, dependability is at the middle level, and in the third, internalization is at the highest level. Bowles and Gintis phrase it "similarly in education." They mention examples of high school, community colleges, and four-year colleges as corresponding respectively to the three different models of the organization of work.

We can imagine our own examples. Even within a single school, different age-grades might reflect different degrees of freedom. Or, schools that are at the same formal level, say high schools, can organize the teaching and learning process very differently. The hypothesis from my own empirical research that was influenced by the Marxist tradition's emphasis on social class differences showed how high school social life and experience can be very differently structured, depending on the social class context of the school and its teachers and students. Indeed, as we shall soon see from that example, the relation between social class and personal development is an interactional process—one where different schools shape different types of individual identities.

The study of identity and experience in school has long been the province of anthropology of education. While there is now a stream of critical anthropology, the anthropology of the school has ordinarily been a Durkheimian anthropology, either structuralist or functionalist. Willis's empirical study of the everyday life of a group of teenaged schoolboys in England is a leading example of how the Marxist interest in social class, cultural reproduction, and education has been extended and enhanced to experience and identity. With Willis and others (see, for example, Foley, 2001), Marxism in Education discovers the classical anthropological and American or Chicago-school style of "ethnography" and "fieldwork." Bowles and Gintis used quantitative measures and statistical tests of personal and organizational characteristics to understand structural correspondences between school and work. Willis has the same interest, but, as a field researcher with an interest in how people find meaning in their everyday lives, he observes, listens, talks, and interviews in order to grasp the "gestalt" or total way of life of the "participants."

Interestingly, field researchers, even if they are doing this sort of ethnographic work, who are influenced by Marxist theory do not write so much as Althusser and Bourdieu do about "agents." They are more interested in "subjects," in people and their experiences. But, these researchers are also interpreting, listening, and observing the subjects or participants in the framework of a set of concepts or theories about the social process of education. "Critical ethnography" (Carspecken, 1999) is this style of research where the conceptual framework is drawn from the tradition of Marxist social theory.

Willis reports on the specialized vocabulary that his subjects use, on their specific culture. So, for example, he uses the term

"have a laff" to mean the participants' way of describing some of their activities that are amusing, subverting, and inciting. This activity has meaning in the lives of the boys—a meaning that Willis interprets in terms of his Marxist theory of what the activity means. His theoretical interest, as with Apple, Anyon, and Bowles and Gintis, is to explore the relation between the economy and the school. More specifically, he is interested in reproduction, especially the reproduction of labor power.

The main line of his interpretation of the boys' activities in school is that they are in opposition or "resistance" to the dominant culture that is represented by the school, particularly by the teacher-student relationship. Their opposition to the authority of the teachers is an opposition to control over their personal space, their freedom of movement, as well as their more "symbolic space," to create a cultural world that is meaningful to them. The similarity to Bowles and Gintis, despite the many differences in locale and research method, is in the relation between the culture of the school and the social relations of production, particularly the world of work. As Willis phrases it (1977; 39): "there are also many profound similarities between the school counter-culture and shop-floor culture."

He tries to show how the use of the "informal" social life of the school as a place to reclaim the authority of the formal that it experiences as oppressive is a process of cultural creation. The boys, or "lads," to use a research term, opt for all sorts of activities to get out of class. They are also trying to show how masculine they are and to enhance their self-esteem in general through sexist as well as racist sentiments and actions. So many of these activities are reminiscent, according to Willis, of the adult workplace. The attempt to reclaim personal mobility by creating an anti-school culture that borrows its elements from male working class culture is parallel to a social process that occurs in production: "the massive attempt to gain informal control of the work process" (Willis, 1977; 53).

The boys, as Willis puts it, are "learning to labour." While their opposition to the formal authority and organization of the school has elements of an insightful social criticism, a criticism of the class character of schooling, ultimately it contributes to their "learning to labour." For what they are learning in their informal oppositional behavior is not how to get ahead in the middle class world, but how to prepare themselves—in ways that include the cultural skills that enable both opposition and personal survival—for adult life in the working class world of work of their family origins.

This then is an empirical study of reproduction. It is different methodologically, though, because we enter into the everyday experiences, activities, and processes of constructing meanings that organize the lives of the participants. It is different also theoretically. In many ways, the study shows how people, in this case, students in school, contest the dominant culture that is being reproduced. They are not simple "agents of the structure" who are "being interpellated." They are lively social actors, subjects, real people, who are making their lives. Of course, they are not "making it just as they please." The functioning of the structure of class reproduction is seen as more complex and certainly as less direct.

The theoretical irony and difference of this research is that class reproduction that operates through experienced cultural creativity and opposition to the culture of the ruling class does not happen by submitting to authority and internalizing its cultural definitions. Rather, it is in the very process of resisting and opposing the dominant institutional class culture of the school that the boys do the cultural and personal informal educational "work" of cultural class reproduction. They learn to labor, that is, they learn the working class's way of working. They "feed" themselves into the apparatus of class reproduction because the way that they resist is to recreate the culture of the less powerful, dominated working class. Resistance is a method of cultural reproduction and helps replicate the wider social structure of capitalist society.

Willis (2000) was influenced by cultural and literary schools of scholarship and research, as well as by Marxism. My research in schools is significantly influenced by Frankfurt School critical theory. However, more like the other American and English researches whom we have introduced with the Marxist model, I have tried to study social class differences. My own "ethnographic" work includes several different field research studies, but here I want to highlight studies of different high schools located in different geographical and socioeconomic or social class sections of the same city (Wexler, 1992). Like the Frankfurt School,

however, I am interested in social psychology, particularly in a critical social psychology (Wexler, 1990).

Marxist Interactionism

I have taken two roads to "bringing Marx down to earth." Marx was, of course, ultimately concerned about the nature of everyday life. But his socioeconomic theory, as an attempt to understand how and why inequality and suffering are determined by social and economic organization, is a theory about the dynamics of social structure. In my book *Critical Social Psychology* (1983, 1996), I tried to show how his structuralist analysis could also become more sociopsychological. Unlike the Frankfurt School social psychology, I did not directly try to combine Freud with Marx. Instead, I asserted that Marx's theory is already a social psychology, if it could only be understood that way (1996; 81):

> Marxist categories make better sense of the character of contemporary interactions than do the ultimately psychologically ideologizing and reductionist concepts of various versions of market or romantic individualism and conservative organicist social theories. A first step in developing a critical social psychology which draws from the Marxist tradition is to generalize these relational categories. (Wexler, 1981a)

I suggest that we generalize the categories of alienation, commodification (commodity fetishism), and exploitation, not as abstract social structures (society) or as personalized traits (the individual), but as interactional processes.

A Marxist interactionism means studying the actual social interaction among people, but from the viewpoint of Marx's understanding of how the overall society is organized or structured, and how it works or functions. It also means that although the category of "culture" is important, and certainly in the Marxism in Education that focuses on "cultural reproduction," it is not enough to describe social structure and culture. We need to be able to describe day-to-day relations between people in general and, given our interest, between people in schools in particular. Structure and culture set the framework and give us an understanding of the whole, what is sometimes called "the macro." My view is that while we should not forget the context in which interactions occur, we must also not forget the interactions themselves, the level of "the micro."

The move toward Marxist interactionism and "critical ethnography" is a way of underlining that in terms of research practice. Economic structure, cultural reproduction, and correspondences between work and school are all valuable applications of Marxist social theory to education. Ethnographic or field research in education is an attempt to get at the actualization of the social lives that are formed by structure, culture, and correspondence in organization among different sectors of society, especially work and school.

The first road to doing that is to recall that Marx's theory is a theory of general social processes. We have discussed alienation and exploitation as the loss of control in the labor process and as the partial and limited return for labor. Commodification refers to the process by which every aspect of social life becomes like objects that are produced for sale and profit in the marketplace. As we briefly mentioned, Marx referred to that process as "commodity fetishism." The commodity, or the object that is produced for exchange purposes, is like a fetish or idol, because the energy and power of labor that made it is forgotten and all the "power" of human labor is shifted to its product, the commodity—at least in our minds.

From the vantage-point of Marxist social theory, we began to understand the school as a place where we not only "learn to labour," but we actually do labor. If learning can be thought of as working, then it is not only a matter of economic influences on schooling, or cultural and economic reproduction, or correspondences in social organization. Rather, the socioeconomic, dynamic-structured processes described by Marx actually occur in the course of students' activities while they are in school. Lave and McDermott (2003) have made an effort to read Marx's text very closely and to show how we can get a good portrait of the school by substituting the word "learning" for "labor." More practically, we can begin to understand the grades-directed character of learning as an example of commodification, and the instrumental character of the student-teacher relation as an element in the alienation of the student from his/her own learning power and control over the learning process.

A Marxist framed "micro," or small-scale interactionism, is a complement to structuralism and culturalism of "macro" Marxist theories of society that have been applied to education.

This interactionist interest in the social processes of capitalism as typifying school life is the first "road" to "bringing Marx down to earth," or at least to bringing Marx's theory of society to education.

The second road is to recall the importance in this tradition of socially structured inequality. As we discussed briefly, social differences are structured according to what is most important in this theory of social structure: position in the economic process—more precisely, position in social relation to the process of production. If production is the determining feature of organized society, then production location should have wide-ranging effects.

We already know that what matters for this location in production, within a capitalist society, is ownership of the means of production, which includes the whole apparatus of production, including technology. These organized locations are social classes. In capitalism, there is a process of reduction or polarization of classes. Increasingly then, society is divided between the owners and the workers, the capitalist and the proletariat. This is a stark view of social class.

Studies of social differences and inequality in education (Hallinan, 2000) are generally researched with a less sharply divided view of social classes. Inequality is a continuum along a number of dimensions, including differences in income, education, social prestige, and other social attributes. This emphasis on "socioeconomic status" is what prevails, much more than the Marxist idea, in empirical studies of inequality in education.

After all, Marx's theory does not work out the meaning of class differences in all the specific social institutions, including education. Nevertheless, the core idea, which is more strongly coded in Marxism, is that social class position determines many other aspects of a person's life. To study that educationally, from a Marxist and interactionist view, I applied a modified Marxist version of economic social class to differences, not among individuals, but among schools. In *Becoming Somebody* (1992; see also 2007), I wanted to know how it is to live school life in different social classes.

My focus combined this interest in social class with descriptions of social interaction and how, together, that mattered for identity—not only for how students in the three high schools that

I studied defined themselves, but also for identity as intimately related to the way that schools of different social classes structure social interaction. We have several interrelated aspects: social class, social interaction, and identity. In this particular study, I studied three social classes. The professional middle class school was not what traditional Marxism would acknowledge as a school for the capitalist class. I might have found other schools, particularly private schools, where the parents of most of the students were owners of capital. However, in contemporary capitalism, the upper echelons of the professional middle class have a certain amount of power and wealth, in what has become a more complex production process, different from the industrial capitalism that Marx described. One school, however, does represent the more traditional working class, where many of the parents work on the assembly line of a mega-factory. At the same time, especially in the Unites States, class is deeply intertwined with race. I used the term "urban underclass" to describe a school where many of the students came from Afro-American and Hispanic families living in economically depressed parts of the city, where high rates of unemployment is common.

In this model, education is a class process. Race and ethnicity are intertwined with class, and gender makes a difference in all the schools, across classes, although perhaps in different ways. The class process of education means that the life-worlds of teenagers in high schools are very different. We talk about "high school" or "teenagers" as if they were unified categories. In this ethnographic research, we can see how, despite obvious similarities between "school" and "teenager," across the class divide, the character of their everyday lives in school is different, depending on where they are in the social class structure.

Preoccupations of people, both students and teachers, are different. They may have the same curriculum—although often they do not, and it may be taught differently—but they do not have the same concerns. Here, I just want to give a few examples to make the point that school life is life in class society—in race and gender society, as well. Here, in the Marxist model, I want to emphasize the class character of lived schooling.

For example, in the urban underclass school, students struggle with an overall deprecation and devaluation of their self-worth. Not that there is a conscious conspiracy of the school against the

students. On the contrary, there are many dedicated professionals who want their students to learn and succeed and who are themselves Afro-Americans, or Whites who have no racial prejudice. Rather, the school is structured in a way that communicates a lack of confidence in the students' worth, their value as "somebody."

One of the strengths of ethnographic research in Education is that the ways in which this structuring of school life actually happens can be described in detail and with examples from the people who are living that life. Here, we are not going to go into the ethnographic details of "thick description." We do, however, want to have some sense of what difference social class makes in the way that school life is lived by teenagers.

The devaluation and even the "attack" on the identity value of students lead them to find ways to reassert their value, to show that they are indeed "somebody." Part of their identity work in school is to display their worth by whatever cultural means that are available to them. Still, the self is under siege.

The students in the working class school feel less attacked by the school authorities. It is more that many report a lack of "care" about them, an indifference of the school toward them. Here, there is a much less unified view of students versus school, in part because there are so many differences and divisions among the students themselves. In our research, we found a "divided self," where students were torn not only between different peer groups but also between divided aspects of the school organization, particularly between a more "caring" therapeutic" orientation and a more discipline- and punishment-centered way of organizing the students' lives. Unlike Willis's study, where the school sets the basic terms for opposition and the students seem to do the rest, we saw how much of the ongoing daily life of students is influenced by the overall class-related models of the school structure.

Children of the professional middle class went to a much newer, more pleasant school, in a greener and more affluent neighborhood. Their concerns were different and the identity dynamics that emerged in their school interactions were different. They are not coping so much with attacks on the very value of their self, which leads to a compensating set of strategies of a "displayed self." Nor are they living in a clearly divided school, structurally polarized beyond the usual peer group differences, which leads them to a "divided self" and the creation of mere images of unity. Rather, they are subject to pressures for performance, for individual distinction that is so much emphasized that they cannot easily locate the collective social nature of school life, even as they are all "there," together. Instead, faced with continuous and what they perceive as accelerating demand for performance and academic achievements, they try to tune down, to depress the pressure—to the point of becoming apathetic and of producing a "depressed self."

This is only an example, only a report that barely skims the surface of the possible detailed descriptions of social interaction and identity in class schools of what might be called a "critical ethnography." For Marxist social theory in Education, there is an interactionist as well as a structuralist and culturalist point of view. What these different perspectives have in common is a critical theory of society based in Marx. Although later than Durkheimian theory in Education, Marxist theory in Education has spawned a number of empirical researches and a diversity of style of work that represent different theoretical emphases.

This Marxist tradition in Education continues, particularly in the work of theorists and practitioners of "critical pedagogy" (McLaren and Kincheloe, 2007). Here, Marx's adage that "philosophers have only interpreted the world; the point is to change it" is applied to education. Inspired particularly by the educational theory and practice of Paula Freire, critical pedagogy aims to change teaching into a broader approach to inducing social change by an empowering of learners to social awareness. In a way, this is reminiscent of Marx's concept of a "class for itself." Not only social position in production, but consciousness of one's position and the working of the capitalist society in which one is embedded too is a necessary ingredient in altering an unjust society.

From structure to culture to interaction to pedagogy, Marxist social theory in Education continues to influence the way we think and act educationally, even as the forces of production change. As we move from an industrial society to an informational society, division, inequality, domination, and opposition also continue—from the factory floor to a globalized marketplace.

Glossary

Commodity—A key concept for Marx, indicating products that are made for sale, rather than for use by its producers or

workers. Commodity fetishism means that people who make the products and certainly those who consume them lose sight that the products embody the efforts, the work of the producers. Ultimately, we attribute all power to the commodity and none to the producer. Commodification means that not only economic production of things, but also all other aspects of social life, such as friendship, family, and learning, take on the form of the commodity.

Domination—A term used by the Frankfort School of Critical Theory to indicate that submission to the will of others is not just based on forceful power. Deep power is reinforced by belief or culture and psychology. In Critical Theory, the working class remains dominated, accepting its condition in part because of the effectiveness of the power of mass culture. Domination is similar to Weber's concept of "authority," where people obey because they believe that it is right. The reasons for their belief are different and include the traditional, the rational, and the charismatic.

Ethnography—A style of research, originally from Anthropology, that in doing social analyses pays special attention to the people's or participants' own views and ways of life. In Education, it is sometimes called "qualitative research," to differentiate it from statistical methods of social analysis. Critical ethnography is a more specialized term that aims to signal that the theory behind the observations of "real" people in their "natural" settings is derived from Marxism and Critical Theory. Critical ethnography has interests that are not only descriptive and explanatory but also value-based and social change-oriented.

Mode of Production—Marx uses the term to refer to the overall social and economic organization of the work process in which people produce what they need to live ("use") as well as to what is produced for the marketplace and profit ("exchange"). The mode of production includes the forces of production—especially technology and the social processes closest to it; and the social relations of production, which includes not only property ownership, but also most other political and social arrangements. One of Marx's hypotheses is that the forces of production change faster than the social relations of production. This conflict, within the structure, basically between technology and property relations, is what leads classes to act and to cause fundamental revolutionary social changes.

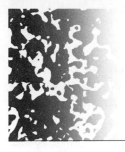

CHAPTER FOUR

Weberian Social Theory in Education

Weber's theory has had no such influence in Education. It has been suggested that we could see Weber as a bridge to postmodern society and its social theories (2005). I have written about Weber in relation to the emergence of the "new age" (Wexler, 2007c). Weber himself wrote at least partly in dialogue with Marx in an effort to create what he saw as a more complex understanding of the multiple causes operating to shape social life.

Weber's Niche

Weber has had less influence on social theories in education because he was outside of the dynamic opposition between Durkheimian Functionalism and Marxist Structuralism, two theories that for so long dominated the social theoretic discourse in Education. He was "the other." Now, however, the social context has changed. Society has itself become more complex and our willingness to recognize multiplicity in all forms has grown. We have become "multicultural," at least ideally, and are interested in the "otherness" of the other," of what is different from us and unfamiliar. Postmodernism welcomed multiplicity.

Spirituality

An exceptionally fashionable and almost indefinable contemporary term that is the source of much disagreement. The overall meaning is to indicate the nonmaterial, the nonsensual, the nonrational, and the experiential interest in inner emotional life that is oriented to what some call the "soul."

Disenchantment and Re-enchantment

This Weberian dynamic is about evolution from a culture of magic and spirits inhabiting the everyday world and making it work, toward a rational or calculative, rule-governed world. That is the disenchantment, the "world robbed of gods," in Weber's term. The re-enchantment is more our term for expressing the possibility that Weber noted, but not hopefully, about the return of magic, spirit, and prophecy to the world. In such a world, "charisma" would be more important than specialized technical knowledge as the basis of social authority.

Weber's difference, and the niche that makes him important for us now, is that his theory of society is so extensively rooted in religion and in the importance of the irrational determinants of social life. Religion is what is different, what is "totally other," from everyday life. Marx dismissed religion as an illusory, disempowering and old-fashioned way of relating to the world. Durkheim took religion seriously. But he came to religion later on in his work, looking for a solution to the de-socializing, fragmenting problem of modern social structure. In searching for the regenerative sources of socially regulative and integrative morality, he focused on religion. His ideas of religion, although it certainly included religious ideas as "collective representations," did largely dismiss the psychological, subjective face of religion. What mattered most, and what ultimately served as a model for all social relations, was religious practice, ritual: doing together.

Why should religion be important to us? Because it is. What that means in Marxist terms is that we need to pay attention to historically changing empirical events and not just keep our vision focused on our theoretical concepts. We have to think from the "ground up," to pay attention to what matters to people. Despite sociological prognostications about the decline of religion, in the view that the modern social world is a secular, nonreligious world, we see a resurgence, a revival of religion. Not only that, we also do not see a general resurgence of the same forms of religion. Church attendance is not up. What we do see are new forms of religion, an "invisible religion" (Luckmann, 1967), an "unchurched" (Wuthnow, 1998) religion, a "holistic" religion (Heelas and Woodhead, 2005). It can also be argued that we see another form of religion that is more fundamentalist and reasserts even more strongly the older models of belief and practice (Castells, 1997).

In either case—and here I am more interested in the first type—Weber's social demands attention to religion in society. The reason that I say that I am more interested in the first case has to do with Weber's understanding of religion. Religion begins and ends in magic. Once the world was enchanted, magical, **spiritual**. The history of modern culture is one of disenchantment, the loss of magic. Weber is relevant for the first type of "holistic" or "spiritual" religion because he raises the possibility of a re-enchantment, and a return to a cultural world before it was "robbed of gods."

This re-enchantment, the search for spiritual meaning in everyday life is what lies at the core of the "new age" and "spiritual movements." We are not so much engaged in a quest for certainty as in a quest for meaning and experience. Part of the quest is in returning a magical, non-calculative, non-instrumental, less practical element to everyday life. Weber inquired about the opposition between what we earlier referred to as the "two cultures," in relation to education—the rational and spiritual.

Part of the theoretical and research work that I think remains ahead of us is, of course, to continue and modify the Durkheimian and Marxist traditions of theory in Education. But the biggest challenge may be to develop a Weberian dynamic theory. Not the dialectical dynamic of class conflict or the dynamic conflict between forces and relations of production. Instead, the conflicting and creative dynamic of a dialectic between the rational and the irrational, between disenchantment and re-enchantment, becomes our main question. We want to ask what that now means for education and what it will mean in the future.

Disenchantment and Re-enchantment

We started with the view that we need to think about social theory not only in relation to theoretical traditions and durability and continuity, but also in relation to the historical social context and its "problematic." The central problem of modern society for Weber is the triumph of bureaucratic rationality and all that it does to the human spirit. Weber is also a social critic, like Marx, and indeed, like Durkheim. His is not a criticism of alienation, exploitation, and commodity fetishism, or a criticism of anomie and excessive individualism. His criticism is of rationalization and intellectualization. Our social evolutionary advance has been from magic to spirits, and then to the organized religion of cults and priests, interspersed with dissenting prophets, but moving always onward toward a non-spiritual way of life that dries us up and makes us more like stones than living beings. This is a deep social criticism of the modern world and an identification of its main social process. Weber explains (1946; 139):

> The increasing intellectualization and rationalization do not, therefore, indicate an increased and general knowledge of the conditions under which one lives.

Rough Translation: We are not getting smarter.

He continues:

> It means something else, namely the knowledge or belief that if one but wished, one could learn it any time. Hence it means that principally there are no mysterious incalculable forces that come into play, but rather that one can, in principle, master all things by calculation. This means that the world is disenchanted. One need no longer have recourse to magical means in order to master or explore the spirits, as did the savage, for whom such mysterious powers existed. Technical means and calculations perform the service. This is above all what intellectualization means. Now, this process of disenchantment.

And what does that mean? Gerth and Mills provide an excellent guide to Weber (1946; 50):

> Weber thus identifies bureaucracy with rationality, and the process of rationalization with mechanism, depersonalization, and oppressive routines.... He deplores the type of man that the mechanization and the routine of bureaucracy selects and forms. The narrowed professional.

The disenchantment or de-magification of religion is a general social and cultural phenomenon, going way beyond evolutionary changes in the character of religion. It is "the world" that is disenchanted. It is "the world" that has been de-magicified and "robbed of gods." This historical change is a change in culture. It is a change in beliefs. In a complex world, although beliefs cannot be the only factor, they are a major factor in shaping our actions. Indeed, Weber is the theorist of social action. Social action is not just acting or behaving. It is taking account of the other and the meaning of one's own action. Culture provides the meaning. If culture becomes more calculating and less spiritual, then action loses its vital force. That is because religion stands behind culture. As Weber puts it (1958; 183):

> The modern man is in general, even with the best will unable to give religious ideas a significance for culture and for national character which they deserve.

Against Marx, Weber reasserts the causal power of ideas in society, not just economic production, but more. The ideas that really count are religious ideas, because it is religious ideas, his work shows, that have a special "significance for culture."

The reach of culture and religious ideas extends from the intellectualization and rationalization of magic to the most powerful social organizational form of modern society: bureaucracy. Rationalization is most clearly expressed in the prevalence of bureaucracy in society, that is, it the prevalence of bureaucrats, experts, and professionals as social types or, as he put it, "characters."

This is a different model of how society works than either Durkheim's or Marx's social structural emphasis. Culture leads to structure, although, of course, Weber would want to have qualified such a general statement in his view of multi-causality in a more complex world. Still, bureaucracy is the social organizational form that most embodies the cultural evolution toward rationalization and intellectualization, and away from magic and the spiritual world. Bureaucracy has its virtues, and there are social, functional reasons that it prevails in the modern world (Weber, 1946; 214):

> The fully developed bureaucratic mechanism compares with other organizations exactly as does the machine with the nonmechanical modes of production.

Rough translation: Marx was right, but he forgot to talk about the form of social organization that is central to modern life—bureaucracy. Like capitalism, there are reasons for its success. Weber continues (214):

> Precision, speed, unambiguity, knowledge of the files, continuity, discretion, unity, strict subordination., reduction of friction and of material and personal costs—these are raised to the optimum point in the strictly bureaucratic administration.

Weber is also providing a social psychology. Actually, he is providing two social psychologies, one, as we shall see, links religious belief directly with character or personality types. Religion creates an ethos, a set of dispositions, a "habitus," or individual, but socially shared, psychology. The other social psychology is an organizational social psychology of a more social structural sort, almost reminding us of Althusser's structuralist Marxist view of education as a state apparatus and the "interpellation of the subject." Weber attributes great power to the bureaucratic form of social organization that can shape its social subjects (216):

> The more complicated and specialized modern culture becomes, the more its external supporting apparatus demands the personally detached and strictly "objective" expert, in lieu of the master

of the older social structures, who was moved by personal sympathy and favor, by grace and gratitude. Bureaucracy offers the attitudes demanded by the external apparatus of modern culture in the most favorable combinations.

It is important to recognize Weber's criticism, both from a general social point of view and also because it gives us a hint about his understanding of education in society. Weber is not neutral. He does provide long analyses about the dangers of overly politicizing social analyses. But he certainly has a particular "judgment," although he says we shouldn't judge about the types of people who are created out of the culture of rationalization and the social structure of bureaucracy. He famously describes this modern world as an unfriendly place, an "iron cage," and calls us "modern persons." He writes (1958; 182):

> No one knows who will live in this cage in the future, or whether at the end of this tremendous development entirely new prophets will arise, or there will be a great rebirth of old ideas and ideals, or, if neither, mechanized petrification, embellished with a sort of convulsive self importance.

Translation: We're full of it.

He goes on to describe the modern person, the final product of this culture and society:

> For of the last stage of this cultural development, it might well be truly said: "Specialists without spirit, sensualists without heart; this nullity imagines that is has attained a level of civilization never before achieved."

Rough translation: We think we're great. Really, we're just zeroes, nobodies. More seriously, he is describing the personal costs of the creation of modern society. This modern society also has a typical religion and a typical and parallel education. We want to describe these social patterns of the rationalized, disenchanted society and then ask what is it that Weber offers as hints to an alternative, to a re-enchantment. It is those hints that speak to a social world beyond the modern, to a new, spiritual age, of which perhaps Weber was a forerunner.

Religion and Education

Religion and education belong to the same historical dynamic. That dynamic is evolutionary and conflictual. The evolution of education is not much described by Weber, although he has a few words to say about it, and we will quote him directly. Here too, as with Marx, part of the importance of learning classical social theory in education is in going back to the original textual sources. Mostly, in this book, I give you my reading of the sources and my comments. But, I think it is valuable for young scholars to learn to form their own readings and interpretations. So, to an extent I have tried to present Durkheim and Marx in their own words. Weber's words are sometimes complex, and I offer succinct "translations." Remember that complexity is one of the ways of doing social theory that Weber admires. He wants us to think in terms of multiple causes of phenomena.

In *The Protestant Ethic and the Spirit of Capitalism* (1958), his most famous book, he takes pains to assure the reader that he is not just going to turn Marx upside down and give pride of causal place to ideas and consciousness instead of production and economics. Here is how he puts his methodological position (1958; 90–91):

> For we are merely attempting to clarify the part which religious forces have played in forming the developing web of our specifically modern culture, in the complex interaction of innumerable historical factors.

He reiterates his position with the phrase "countless historical circumstances."

This well-known book is part of Weber's much larger work on the sociology of religion. Like Marx, he does not have an explicit social theory of education. Yet, just as Marx's theory of social production yielded a rich harvest and vibrant tradition of social theory and research in Education, Weber's theory of religion in society has at least the potential to serve as a springboard for such a tradition. So far, Weberian social theory is least developed in education. We can make a beginning by showing the parallels between religion and education for Weber and by seeing how we might create a fuller Weberian social theory of education.

Weber's theory of religion in society is evolutionary. He tried to go back to the earliest history in order to explain how we got to where we are now, to the modern European context in which he lived and wrote. The earliest forms of religion are magical, with people trying to induce unseen forces and spirits to help them in

being more effective in the world (Weber, 1978). Religion has an interest in this world. Over time, interest in a world inhabited by concrete spirits becomes more abstract, eventually leading to belief in gods. This is the process of intellectualization that he described. It begins in religion, but it becomes an ever more general social process. We try to influence the gods by our practices, which become organized as religious cults and churches. At the same time, we develop more abstract, general ideas about these unseen religious forces. Magic and spirit increasingly recede, in favor of organized religion and systems of religious ideas.

That is the overarching historical trend: intellectualization and rationalization. That is the disenchantment or, more precisely, the de-magification of the world. This process is, naturally for Weber, complex. There is more than one road taken under the big umbrella of the move away from an enchanted world. Two things happen that are important in understanding modern religion. While it is true that people are trying to accomplish similar things by religion, they do it in different ways. What we are trying to accomplish is to make sense of our lives, to give meaning to the world. That is why Weber's German term "verstehen" is so often cited as a key to his methodology and his theory. It means understanding. Weber's research principal was that we could study social action only by "understanding" what it means to the participants.

We are trying to make sense of the world to develop a system of meanings, a "theodicy." We want to explain many things, particularly death and suffering, but also why some people have good fortune in life. We want to justify or "rationalize" our existential situation. In addition to giving meaning to our actions and our situation, we also try to enhance our experience. Religion, in ways not dissimilar to the "collective effervescence" produced in Durkheim's description of religious ritual assemblies, is about "ecstasy," about special and intense experiences. Religion then aims to give meaning and experience. Ultimately, what we are looking for is some sort of salvation from this world.

There are different "roads to salvation," as Weber put it. One way, the most famous in Weber's description of the Protestant ethic, is to try to get some sign that we are actually going to be saved, that we have "grace." If we act ethically in the world and control the satisfaction of our impulses, this might be considered

Asceticism

Weber uses the terms to describe an orientation in religious practice that is based on denial of the pleasures of the senses, and on extreme self-discipline. The importance of this way of acting is that the ascetic path toward finding salvation is the source of the Protestant Ethic. This is the package of culture and psychology that creates the culture of the modern world that Weber called the "spirit of capitalism" The ascetic character is the ancestor of the expert and professional type who embody rationality and rule the modern world.

Mysticism

A very general term that includes many different views of religion. For Weber, the emphasis is on contemplation rather than on action, on inward rather than outward, on escaping from the social world rather than being engaged by it. He does describe it also in ways that others use it, namely, to indicate the search for unity between the individual and the transcendental or cosmic dimension.

a sign of our already decided fate of being saved. One never knows, but ethical conduct and its reward is a reflection of living as an instrument of an invisible but powerful god. This way of living, that of an **ascetic**, a person who denies satisfying all of his or her sensual desires, is a highly organized, careful and methodical way of life. Weber observes (1978; 544): "A person who lives as a worldly ascetic is a rationalist." This is a "man of vocation." This is the character type that has built the modern capitalist order.

That is Weber's great irony, and maybe it is his reply to Marx. People who were religious Protestants, in trying to reach salvation by becoming ethical and self-denying or "ascetic," contributed to the development of an economic system. The economic aspect of society is influenced by the cultural, and ultimately by religion. Even after people stopped having the religious beliefs that led them to ascetic behaviors, they continued that way of life, that social character, that set of dispositions or "habitus"—a continuance of that makes capitalism work. It is its "spirit." A religious ethic influences a secular, economic ethic and helps to make the culture and character of modern capitalism.

That is only one road to salvation. The other is to try to reunify the older, magical spirit world that has now been split into rational cognition and religious beliefs. The way to do that is not by acting ethically and showing your obedience to god, in the hope that such action is a sign of salvation. The way to do that is by contemplation, even meditation, we would say now. Not acting, but contemplating and trying to find those meanings and experiences that will reunify the world. To find, in Weber's terms, "a unity beyond all empirical reality." This is the "inward" life. This is the life that does not engage the economic world and help to create the culture of capitalism. It does not change a religious ethos into an economic spirit. It leaves the world and "flees" from economic activity. This is the **mystical** solution to the search for salvation.

There are, of course, mystics in the modern world. But they are not the dominant social character and theirs is not the dominant culture. The prevailing culture is the culture of the religious ascetic who in becoming secular and has taken that religious energy, that drive for activity, and directed it toward economic success. The ascetic has become the modern rationalist, the "man

of vocation," the expert, the bureaucrat and the professional. We see how, in this famous example, the religious quest in ideas and experience stands behind culture and the modern personality type.

This development—the quest for religious salvation that leads to the dominant secular culture of rationalist capitalism—is one important thing that happens. The other thing is that the mystical impulse also has a history. It is rooted in "charisma," grace, or a certain personal magnetism that some people have. Charisma is a version of early magic, that is, special powers. Now, while Weber thought that the world had become mostly disenchanted, occasionally, this magical gift of grace, the power of charisma, returns to society. Early in history, we have magicians, later, prophets, still later, various secular leaders. Weber does not necessarily like all of these new leaders, but he cannot deny their power to draw and mobilize social action, to become the basis of social authority. This magical charismatic force breaks out from time to time and changes history.

Rationalization that comes from magic/charisma is the leading force. But the old force, in different forms, comes back to challenge it. Society is indeed conflicted, though not by social classes. The conflict in society is between cultural principles and ways of life. Our earlier quotes from Weber about us being a "nullity" or nobodies shows that he does not like the victory of rationalization over charisma. But, he does not deny the historical reality of rational authority, nor the prevalence of its organizational form—bureaucracy—nor the type of person characteristic of our times—the expert. Weber's hope for charisma can be seen in these excerpts about charisma, which (Weber, 1947; 361, 362, 328):

> is thus specifically outside the realm of everyday routine and the profane sphere…repudiates the past, and is in this sense a specifically revolutionary force…The concept of "charisma" ("the gift of grace") is taken form the vocabulary of early Christianity.

The Education Part of the Story

Weber, as we mentioned, has much less to say about education than he does about religion. Although he does write about it, he does so only sparsely and produces nothing like the detailed evolutionary history of religion, his sociology of religion. Education represents the same cultural conflict as in religion. There are scattered comments in *Economy and Society* (1978), Weber's magnum opus, about how education is related to the culture of different groups, of warriors and priests, and about how it has undergone a historical evolution. But his main comments are about contemporary education.

In education, the cultural conflict between the principles of rationalization and charisma, and the triumph of bureaucratic, expert rationalistic society, mirrors the victory of ascetic rationality over contemplative mysticism and charismatic magic. These are two cultural clusters and they are at war with each other in modern society. Weber knows, unhappily, which side is winning.

First of all, education is a cultural question. It is not primarily about economic production and class position, nor about integrating sociality and collective assemblies. It is about our cultural commitments, our ideals about ways of being in the world, ways of life. Here is what he has to say about the contemporary education in the modern European social context of his times. Significantly, his comment is nested within his larger discussion of bureaucracy (Weber, 1946; 243):

> Behind all the present discussion of the foundations of the educational system, the struggle of the "specialist type of man" against the older type of "cultivated man" is hidden at some decisive point. This fight is determined by the irresistibly expanding bureaucratization of all public and private relations of authority, and the ever-increasing importance of expert and specialized knowledge. This fight intrudes into all intimate cultural questions.

There is one very specific textual source in Weber's discussion of these opposing cultural principles where he does not write just about the older "cultivated" person whom bureaucracy destroyed, wiping out personalistic traditions and replacing them by continuous rational calculation according to rules. Here he reveals his view of the deep cultural divide, the conflict, the duality between charisma and rationalization—between the enchanted world that became disenchanted and might someday be re-enchanted by magic, charisma, and spirit.

In modern culture, the "fight," as he puts it, is pretty much over. There are small pockets of private spirituality, but public society is organized according to heartless and spiritless rules. Yet,

he can observe the opposition as one that has appeared "histori-cally." In a discussion of Confucian education, he raises consider-ation of the different "types" of educational systems, even writing explicitly about this as a sociological approach to education. But, he is quick to say that it is only a hint for us (1946; 426):

> To be sure, we cannot here, in passing give a sociological typol-ogy of pedagogical ends and means, but perhaps some comments may be in place.
>
> Historically, the two polar opposites in the field of edu-cational ends are: to awaken charisma, that is, heroic qualities or magical gifts; and, to impart specialized expert training. The first type corresponds to the charismatic structure of domination; the latter type corresponds to the rational and bureaucratic (modern) structure of domination ….Between them are found all those types which aim at cultivating the pupil for a conduct of life.

He goes on to offer a very concise typology of the aims of education. The aims of education are different and are often in historic conflict. They depend on the form of authority or the kind of meanings that people find most persuasive in a specific social context. Education is historically social because it exem-plifies a broader cultural principle. It expresses and specifies the culture in the domain of teaching and learning—just the way that religion expresses the historic evolution of culture and its unhappy conflicted result. What are the aims of education, "the ends and means," and how are they different? (426, 427).

Charismatic education is connected to the history of ancient magic, sorcerers, warriors, and heroes. What such an education aims to do is "to awaken." Charismatic education awakens what is already present, the "personal gift of grace." It is almost like a practice of rebirth, of acquiring a "new soul." Charismatic education is an awakening of the gifts of the spirit.

Education in the modern bureaucratic society is not awaken-ing, but training. No personal magical gift is required. Like the universality of the bureaucratic administrative order that it serves, "this can be accomplished with anybody." Training is technical. It is practical. It is a preparation to work in administrative organi-zations, in all sectors of society, from business to science to the military. It is a universal education in training to be administra-tively functional, to be useful.

The third type of education is cultivation. Cultivation can also be done with almost anybody, but it is less aimed at imparting technical expertise and useful organizational knowledge. The aim is to teach people about how to act and how to think. It is to form them as a cultural type, appropriate to whatever status for which they are being educated. Marxists might call this "cultural reproduction." Bourdieu would have, I suggest, called it "habitus." It is a certain package of dispositions and traits that enables us to act without thinking in particular cultural contexts. It is part of us, embodied, or, as Weber puts it, the "internal and external deportment in life."

Now, I think, we can understand why if we represent Durkheim in a shorthand way as the social theorist of the social, and if we describe Marx in a condensed way as the social theorist of the economic, Weber is the social theorist of the cultural.

Starting out from Weber

We are not starting out completely from scratch in articulating a Weberian social theory of education. Of course, there is Weberian sociology (Whimster, 2000). There is also research in education that I think we can say is undertaken in the "spirit of Weber." An example is Callahan's (1962) important study of how the idea of efficiency became impressed upon educational thought and practice in the United States in the second decade of the twentieth century. Callahan shows, in a historical study, how a wider social movement, even a "craze," centered around the ideal of efficiency was translated into an educational vision that changed the way that schools were organized and the way teaching and learning were performed. We might even say that he describes in some detail how a general cultural ideal became a set of educational practices that set the stage for education as training. In Weber's typology of pedagogy, there is a shift from cultivation to training.

We can find other examples in the educational literature of work that is "compatible" with Weber's ideas (Hunter, 1994). But, there is no tradition of thinking education socially with Weber's ideas intentionally in mind, the way that there is with the Durkheimian and Marxist traditions of social theory in education. Perhaps, that tradition is now being created. Weber's importance for education is not simply that he shows us how culture is important in social history. Nor is it in his famous analysis of

bureaucracy, or even in the critical tools that his work supplies to educational critics in the analysis of rationalization.

The contemporary importance of Weber for social theory in education lies in his central preoccupation with the disenchantment of the world and the possibilities of re-enchantment. For all his so-called pessimism about the future of modern society, Weber hopes for a resurgence of the spirituality in society that rationalization destroyed (Weber, 1958; 182): "No one knows," he writes, "who live in this cage in the future, or whether at the end of this tremendous development, entirely new prophets will arise, or there will be a great rebirth of old ideas and ideals, or." The hope of this possibility is in itself valuable. It is not an empty hope. Weber has a competing cultural principle against modernity, rationality, bureaucracy, and expertise. He names charisma as a "revolutionary force." The counterculture, which also has an educational application in the practices of "awakening," is the culture of magic, spirit, charisma, and mysticism. Not that Weber easily endorsed these cultural alternatives. He was wary of false prophets and fake prophecies.

The hopeful application of the countercultural principle that, following contemporary popular usage, I would call "spirituality" offers an opening to a different tradition of theory and practice. It is one that stands largely opposed to the rationalist ideal that is embedded in both Durkheim and Marx. The reason that the hope of re-enchantment is engaging is the possibility, as Marx wrote, of us becoming vehicles for the expression of what is happening; theorists can express a changing historical reality, their own cultural context (1956; 66):

> these theorists remain Utopians who...improvise systems...they have no further need to look for a science in their own minds; they have only to observe what is happening before their eyes, and to make themselves its vehicle of expression.

There is growing evidence that one relevant aspect of "what is happening" is what I have called a **re-sacralization** (Wexler, 2000) in society. We can also talk about processes of societal renewal, or "revitalization" (Wallace, 1956). Certainly, not all the evidence is in. There are, however, a number of social theorists and researchers who have analyzed and tried to document a deep cultural shift. Weber's interest in religion as the key to cultural

---

Re-sacralization

Also termed sacralization. It is part of the same dynamic of losing and regaining. The world has "holiness" in it, which both Durkheim and Weber would argue was, at least once, the driving social force. Making the profane or the mundane everyday into something special that members of society worship and stand in awe of is sacralization. Redoing it, for what has already become profane, ordinary, and unholy is re-sacralization.

change and his particular competing cultural principles now seem less and less abstract and out of context.

Social and cultural analysts increasingly focus on new social movements, new forms of meaning and identity, and the important role of spirituality in these historical changes. What we have not yet done, with a few exceptions, is to draw the educational implications from the rise of the new age and the re-enchantment of culture and the resurgence of spirituality. Weber helps point the way both to a general social understanding of these changes, and, as we saw in our discussion of religion and education, to an interrogation of their educational meanings. In that sense, Weber not only stands at the head of the cultural school among the classical sociological theorists whom we are applying to education but also becomes a bridge between the traditions of classical sociology that we have been exploring, to what lies beyond classical sociology.

Glossary

Asceticism—Weber uses the terms to describe an orientation in religious practice that is based on denial of the pleasures of the senses, and on extreme self-discipline. The importance of this way of acting is that the ascetic path toward finding salvation is the source of the Protestant Ethic. This is the package of culture and psychology that creates the culture of the modern world that Weber called the "spirit of capitalism." The ascetic character is the ancestor of the expert and professional type who embody rationality and rule the modern world.

Disenchantment and Re-enchantment—This Weberian dynamic is about evolution from a culture of magic and spirits inhabiting the everyday world and making it work, toward a rational or calculative, rule-governed world. That is the disenchantment, the "world robbed of gods," in Weber's term. The re-enchantment is more our term for expressing the possibility that Weber noted, but not hopefully, about the return of magic, spirit, and prophecy to the world. In such a world, "charisma" would be more important than specialized technical knowledge as the basis of social authority.

Mysticism—A very general term that includes many different views of religion. For Weber, the emphasis is on contemplation rather than on action, on inward rather than outward, on escaping from the social world rather than being

engaged by it. He does describe it also in ways that others use it, namely, to indicate the search for unity between the individual and the transcendental or cosmic dimension.

Re-sacralization—Also termed sacralization. It is part of the same dynamic of losing and regaining. The world has "holiness" in it, which both Durkheim and Weber would argue was, at least once, the driving social force. Making the profane or the mundane everyday into something special that members of society worship and stand in awe of is sacralization. Redoing it, for what has already become profane, ordinary, and unholy is re-sacralization.

Spirituality—An exceptionally fashionable and almost indefinable contemporary term that is the source of much disagreement. The overall meaning is to indicate the nonmaterial, the nonsensual, the nonrational, and the experiential interest in inner emotional life that is oriented to what some call the "soul."

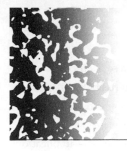

CHAPTER FIVE

Conclusion: Beyond Classical Sociology

My aim in this book has been to introduce the reader to social theory in education. The way that I have chosen to do that is to organize a great deal of work around three central figures in the history of sociological theory, the so-called classical sociology: Durkheim, Marx, and Weber. In each case, we have outlined the basic concepts of each thinker, which taken together form a model or paradigm of society and social processes. We then tried to show how we can use each model to organize a great deal of theory and research in social approaches to Education. We assume that there are certain basic assumptions, key ideas and commitments that characterize each model, and that they form a tradition of work. We can see the influence of the models of classical sociology working many decades after they were first created and in different historical contexts.

The models are not all-inclusive. For instance, among European sociologists of that same "classical" era of the late nineteenth and early twentieth century, we have taken the absolutely most central figures. This does not mean that other sociologists of the period, such as Simmel, for example (Needleman, 2000), are not important. It is true, especially for Durkheim and Marx,

that their enduring influence is not only in social theory, but also in social theory in Education. This is what has been most important for us. There are also traditions of American sociology that, though less influential in sociology and even less in Education, do have implications for social theory in education—implications that we did not develop here (Vidich and Lyman, 1985).

We have sacrificed some in inclusiveness in order to give the reader a clear-cut organization for thinking conceptually about Education in a social way. By focusing on the classical models, I think that we are then able to code, process, and sort new work in social theoretic approaches to education. We have a map.

While it surely can help to have this map and to see the continuities in social theories in Education, there are also discontinuities, differences, and changes that are important. Readers of this book ought to be able to find the similarities and the underlying models, even in theories that seem on the surface very different. Nevertheless, there is no denying the important shifts that have taken place after the modern period in which these classical models were first formulated. Modernity has given way to postmodernity, a later period and cultural movement that also found its way to social theory (Lemert, 1995). Postmodern theory has been accompanied by other vibrant developments in Feminism, in Globalization theory, and in the neighboring field of Anthropology (Ritzer and Smart, 2000; Csordas, 1994). Our bet is still that a solid grounding in the basic models of classical sociology will give the novice analyst the surest footing in venturing forth into making sense of historical cultural changes and the various forms of their expression in theory. The challenge remains the same: what does it mean for helping us to better understand Education socially?

Fundamentalism

A very general and popular term. Here, Castells uses it to try to make sense of social movements. These movements develop in reaction to the disorientation of identity and loss of anchors of meaning because of the new informational economy. Fundamentalism points to the restoration of strong beliefs based on primary identities, such as land or religion, that form new communities. They draw cultural strength and stability by having almost unbreakable, "fundamental" cultural codes of meaning.

Social Movements

This is particularly the case in theory and research that emphasizes study of the "new" social movements in society. The so-called new movements (Melucci, 1994) may not be so new, but at least their historical reassertion has caught the attention of social observers. Analysts of social movements have paid particular attention to the appearance of religious **fundamentalism**, to a variety of social movements focusing on personal identity, among them, especially Feminism.

Readers of *Social Theory in Education* who explore these newer domains of work will usefully, I hope, be in a better position to understand, accept, and also criticize these movements than they would be without the conceptual map of our three models. For example, our readers will immediately be able to place some of the most interesting work on social movements that focuses particularly on various forms of fundamentalism within our traditions. Here is what Castells (1996; 2) writes in his opening paragraph: "A technological revolution centered around information technologies is reshaping, at accelerated pace, the material basis of society…" He continues, "Capitalism itself has undergone a process of profound restructuring."

Unlike Marx, however, Castells goes on to explain fundamentalist religious movement in the new information age, in what has come to be known as the "network society" (3):

> In such a world of uncontrolled, confusing change, people tend to regroup around primary identities: religious, ethnic, territorial, national. Religious fundamentalism…in a world of global flows of wealth, power, and images, the search for identity.

Of course, different than Marx, Castells then develops a typology of identities that he sees as contemporary possibilities. While he does not dismiss religion as an illusion, he does understand religious fundamentalism as a defensive reaction to a changing technology that has deeply affected the overall social organization of society. After paying so much attention to Marx's model, we can see here how the forces of production influence the social relations of production and, further, how instead of social classes and class consciousness, we are now paying attention to identity movements. Fundamentalist movements of identity might be seen as collective responses to newer forms of powerlessness, from the alienation and exploitation of modern capitalism to the defensive identities—not of social classes but of communities, of "communal heavens."

In what we might understand as the language of postmodern, informational Marxism, Castells observes (1997; 66):

> God, national, family, and community will provide unbreakable codes…Eternal truth cannot be virtualized…they cannot be dissolved, lost in the whirlwind of information flows and cross-organizational networks.

Cyber-feminism

A virtual community that expresses a radical transgression of ordinary cultural categories in order to achieve a new social model of a feminist politics by use of the technologies of the Web and the Internet. Kenway and Langmead as well as Gur-Zeev offer analyses of this contemporary political-technological movement.

If Castells reminds us of Marx, Melucci (1994; 1996), another major social theorist of new social movements, evokes a different one of our models (1994; 109):

> We must rethink social action into the process by which meaning is constructed through interaction….It is actors who, though their relations, produce and recognize the sense of what they are doing.

Like Weber, Melucci does not ignore the importance of economic forces in society. Indeed, he begins like Castells, with the importance of new forms of information-based production for wider social changes. The changes that Melucci sees are less linked to the defensive formation of strongly coded communities of identity. On the contrary, the economic change leads toward social opening in new movements of attention to the body, sexuality, health, and spirituality. We may start at the economic infrastructure of informational production, but the social action quickly moves past political economy. This reminds us of how Weber asserted multi-causality and the importance of religion and culture for social and historical change (Melucci, 1994; 109):

> Conflicts move from the economic-industrial system to the cultural sphere. They focus on personal identity, the time and space of life, and the motivation and codes of daily behavior.

(Careful readers might ague that a true Weberian would have said "action," and not "behavior," to underline the importance of subjective meanings). Here too, there is a social psychology and an interactionism that uses economic structuralism only as its springboard, and not as its final destination.

The continuity to Weber extends even to the question of what is the main conflict, the gap of competing cultural principles. For Weber, it was rationalization and charisma. Here is how Melucci sees the conflict of cultural principles (1994; 112):

> A split opens between the realm of instrumental knowledge, which efficiently manipulates the symbolic codes that select, order and direct information, and wisdom, as the integration of meaning into personal experience.

There is a Durkheimian element in all of this work. Like Durkheim, the older regulative order is weakening its moral power and normatively disintegrating. New forms of social integration are created, particularly in the new "religions" of the self that Durkheim called the "cult of the individual."

New age

Another popular term, with cultural dissent about its meaning. On the whole, it refers to new cultural commitments, as we indicated in Hanegraaf's treatment. By talking about an "age," the intention is to signify a very major shift in the culture, generally, away from materialism and rationality toward spirituality.

Revitalization

Wallace defined it centrally as visions or a new way of life. Revitalization movement are social movements that reconfigure the culture and try to reorganize people's everyday meanings and routines in a way that restores cultural confidence and individual motivation. A stressed and dying culture is brought back to life by a newly imagined possibility. Culture and character get new energy, new vitality.

It is difficult to find this element of a restorative Durkheimian Functionalism in Kenway and Langmead's (2000) radical, technology-based "cyber-feminism." Yet, they show how powerful the Durkheimian model can be, even when the social movement that it can help make sense of seems to be the most radical. Cyber-feminism is a "transgressive" movement that calls for violating conventional social norms and categories. As Kenway and Langmead observe, **cyber-feminism** uses the new technology of networks and webs politically. Like Lomsky-Feder, who gave an account of ritual ceremonies as sites for oppositional challenge as well as cultural reinforcement, Kenway and Langmead show how a networked community of avant-garde feminists challenge the most basic assumptions of the culture.

Here, technology does not create an uncertainty leading to the reassertion of fundamentalist forms of solidarity. Rather, it fuels the capacity, as Kenway and Langmead indicate (2000; 525), "in challenging such distinctions as mind and body, human and machine, male and female and real life and simulation and indeed pleasure and danger." Info-technology enables cultural movements that "challenge the boundaries." Cyber-feminism does not shore up identity. It dissolves into "liquid identities," where people can assume various and changing forms of self-definition.

"Liquid identities" and the term "girl power" are oppositional to the conventional culture, but they indicate new, ironic, and unfamiliar forms of social solidarity. Cyber-feminism is an instance of the creation of social solidarity out of the very materials that appear to contradict the idea of social order. It is not, as in the case that Willis presented, that resistance contributes to cultural class reproduction. Rather, in a more complicated way, new rituals of collective assembly are formed at the moment of dissolution of profane everyday life, to generate shared social energy. Cyber-feminism is a case of virtual ritual assembly and shows how anti-identities recharge the collective social battery and generate radically new "collective representations" and a new sociality.

New Age Spirituality

Wallace (1956; 265) defines a **revitalization** movement as:

a deliberate, organized, conscious effort by members of a society to construct a more satisfying culture. Revitalization is thus,

from a cultural standpoint, a special kind of culture change phenomenon.

He condenses the definition (268) as "visions of a new way of life by individuals under extreme stress."

He is interested in how new cultural patterns develop in the process of what he calls "mazeway reformulation." He is analyzing the process of the emergence of new cultures as the result of a process of experiencing stress and dissatisfaction with an old culture. Revitalization is a method by which visions of a new culture are created and eventually stabilized to offer people a less stressful and more satisfying way, or mazeway, of organizing their everyday lives.

There is an emerging and growing trend of research and theorizing about current versions of this process. It centers around the idea that there are enough profound cultural changes going on that we can talk about a "new age" (Heelas, 1996). Heelas acknowledges the ambiguity of the term and offers a succinct definition (15):

> How are we to characterize the New Age Movement? The term "new age"—together with similar formulations such as "new times," "new era" or "new world"—is typically used to convey the idea that a significantly better way o life is dawning.

Heelas's and others' (Heelas and Woodhead, 2005) research shows how much the new age can be understood as centrally a religious change. More accurately, there is a tendency, not always strong and clear, to move away from "religion" as the social location for providing life meaning, to an "un-churched" culture of spirituality. Meaning beyond the everyday that creates what Weber called a "meaningful cosmos" is more and more found by people within themselves, and not in external social forms. The "subjective turn" in the new age culture means a quest for the sort of meaning and experience that Weber described as basic in the formation of the religious basis of modern culture. But the search for meaning and experience does not lead to established religion. Instead, it is a "self spirituality."

The beyond, the more, the different, the other, the transcendental—all terms that point to the location of the religious factor—are found within the person himself or herself. As Heelas and others (Csordas, 1994) have described it, there occurs a "sacralization" of the self. The alternative to everyday life that Durkheim saw in ritual religious assemblies as being "the sacred" is sought for by more people in their inner lives, which has taken on a sort of religious value and quest.

There are several elements to this new age spirituality change. First, after a long period of secularization, people seek meaning again in religion. Second, this is a different sort of religion, less organized and formal, more individual and inward. This is what we ordinarily mean when we talk about spiritual, as opposed to religious. Finally, this change includes a set of ideas and commitments that are different from the reigning culture of modernity. We are no longer talking about the triumph of rationality and bureaucracy. It is different than the counter-modern culture of postmodernity. We are not talking about multiculturalism, difference, plurality, and multiplicity. We are pointing to a new cultural vision.

Wuthnow (1998), in his study of the changing form of religion in America, sums up the change in this way (3): "In brief, I argue that a traditional spirituality of inhabiting sacred places has given way to a new spirituality of seeking." Heelas and Woodhead write about a more "holistic" religion, perhaps even signs of a "spiritual revolution."

In addition to the spiritual quest and the search within oneself as the source of nonrational meaning and experience, the new age entails a different culture, a whole range of different beliefs. Hanegraaf (1998) explored the history of ideas in order to understand the various cultural streams that have contributed to the new age. Among his detailed descriptions there are also efforts to schematically present the difference between the culture of the "old" age and new age beliefs. The opposing cultural elements include: from Newton to Einstein; from parts mentality to wholeness; from rationalism to mysticism; from the moral virtue of obedience to the virtue of creativity; from religion to spirituality; from the ascetic to the aesthetic. "The Age of Aquarius" was only a recent beginning of the new age culture. Hanegraaf traces the origins of these elements of belief. He leads us on a long and interesting journey that reveals the "other side" of the history of European culture. This side is about all that was not vanquished by the victory of Weber's Protestant Ethic, rationalism and the "spirit of capitalism."

New Age spirituality becomes the locus of a broad counter-cultural movement. Following our commitment to understanding social theory in its historical context, I have asked what such a cultural change might mean for the models by which we understand society. And, of course, I have asked what the new social movements and new age spirituality might mean for education (Wexler, 2000, 2007a, 2007b).

Social Movements, New Age Spirituality, and Education

There is a huge silence about Education in these new directions of social theory. Among the rare exceptions, O'Sullivan (1999) introduced a cosmological and ecological dimension to educational critique. Miller and his colleagues (2005) have asked what a "holistic learning" would be like, as opposed to what Sloan, in the same book of readings (Miller et al., 2005), called "the modern assault on being human."

Social movement theory is particularly silent about the implications of social and cultural changes that reach beyond impacting on identity to ask more about the processes of forming, creating, and transmitting identities. While there is an obvious recognition that the collective action of social movements entails a "learning process," exactly what that is and how it happens is not specified.

It remains a challenge to elaborate and enhance the relation between social theory and education in these "changing times." There are paths to be taken from the classical sociology of our three models. Collins' ritual interactionist interpretation of Durkheim and Lomsky-Feder's empirical research on school ceremonies give us good guidelines on how to move the Durkheimian model beyond moral education and socialization. In *Becoming Somebody* (Wexler, 1992), I tried to show what it would mean to do a double translation of Marx.

First, to develop the interactionist meanings of his central structuralist concepts in a critical social psychology. Second, to try to make the critical social psychology do the work of explaining everyday educational life in ways congruent with Marx. Weber, the "other," third term in the narrative of classical sociology, had, as we saw, suggestive insights about the opposition of the cultural principles of rationalization and charisma in education. His "sociological typology of pedagogical ends and means" offers us broad hints on how to study teaching and learning. That typology may prove more fruitful than Bourdieu's suggestion that we analyze pedagogy as "symbolic violence."

Weber's model is rooted in his wider critique of power. It is not enough to understand the application of force and violence in society, though that is surely important. Belief and meaning and how they work to shore up authority, which is legitimate power, press us toward the study of culture—as a key to power. We could also say that putting historical cultural commitments into the present, operating simultaneously, gets us out of a unified, ahistorical, functional systems view.

What would it mean to study teaching and learning in terms of awakening, cultivation, and training? Perhaps more radically (Wexler, 2007c), we could explore the transposition of Weber's sociology of religion to educational settings. What does it mean to study magic, sacrifice, prayer, and prophecy as basic social forms, and to ask how they might appear in the context of education? More broadly, we recall Weber's cultural conflict between rationalization and charisma, and the dynamic back and forth between processes of disenchantment and re-enchantment. Is there an educational aspect of this deep and postmodern cultural process in all the cycles and waves of educational reform movements and pedagogical shifts? Alternatively, we could ask what is prophetic and what is priestly education (although we might find it coded in a secular, rather than traditionally religious, way)?

Classical sociology has not had its last word about contributing to our understanding of education as a social process. Two clear challenges—and I have confidence that there are more—would be to apply the core concepts of social movement theory and new age spirituality theory to understanding education: socially, but perhaps in a different way. For social movement theory, the challenge is to rethink Education out of the "systems and institution" conceptual box and to begin to understand—as Callahan's (1962) example indicated, and as the historical work of Katz (1968, 1971) illustrates—that education could be thought of as a crystallization, a sediment, a remainder of social movements. We need to re-historicize social educational theory. Collective action and all the analytical elements that comprise it

(Melucci, 1996) might be a better way to think about education than either system or structure, or even interaction.

The second challenge is to take seriously the "subjective turn" of new age spirituality. Progressive education child-centeredness and the 1960s style alternative education represented a challenge to the rationalist technicism of an earlier modernity. But what does it mean now to talk about inwardness, about self-spirituality and the sacralization of the self, in an informational, network society? I would say that the focus of critical social theory on students has been in terms of the way they are "agents" or, more true to the theory, "pawns" in the continuous reproduction of a social structure of inequality. Our thought that students can be more consciously active, expressed in the hopes of critical peda-gogy (McLaren and Kincheloe, 2007; Gur-Zeev, 2003, 2007), is largely within a political discourse of liberation. The cultural shift that Melucci described, away from an exclusive emphasis on political economy as being the only "critical," has not yet occurred in Education.

This is the challenge of the student as a subject: neither as the agent of the ideological state apparatus of capitalism, nor as the agent of the ideologies of social mobilization and libera-tion. Spirituality in education means a new subjectivity, both in research and in practice. In research, I have described an "eth-nography of being," borrowing from the newer anthropology of consciousness, experience, and embodiment (Wexler, 2000). It means studying the emotional lives of students, their fantasies and dreams, and the students' body as the site of cultural conflict. In pedagogical practice, we might revisit Buber's (1965) "unity of being" as the educator's goal. Or, we might ask about what new age practitioner movements and their historic sources in classical religions imply for pedagogy, as Ergas does for Yoga philosophy and teaching (2008).

One of the values of our earlier discussion of the context of social theory is that it gives us some perspective on these "new" developments. After all, to a student of Romanticism, the New Age may not be so new after all. The "subjective turn" sounds a lot like an "inner revolution" that Abrams (1971) identifies as central to the Romantic movement. There is also the worrying parallel that in the inner revolution of Romanticism—although it may serve as an opposition and an antidote to a contemporary excess of Enlightenment rationalism—should we speak also of a "new" scientism? Romanticism, in Abrams' account develops as a compensation to political defeat and a retreat to the creativity of inner renewal as the best available option. Are we too in retreat, returning to the religious and the spiritual as a protective countermove against even greater victories of a now global culture of modernity? Do we want, like Toulmin, to skip back a century for moral and cognitive sustenance? Or, like McCarthy, to the glories of ancient Greece?

Nevertheless, however we evaluate our position in the conflicted culture of modernity—even when we think that we are postmodern—there is a great deal of work that remains to be done in the field of social theory in education. It is an open text, an unfinished symphony, an invitation to the reader to become, himself or herself, a social theorist of education. This hopeful attitude toward the future is found in the writings of nineteenth-century American transcendentalist philosophers and poets, and Romantics too, such as Emerson, Thoreau, and Whitman. Against McCarthy's reading of American rationalism, there is another strain in American culture that is not only Romantic but also socially critical. Perhaps we can find our revitalization and reintegration by hearing its voice. Thoreau wrote (1960; 221):

> I do not say that John of Jonathan will realize all this; but such is the character of that morrow which mere lapse of time can never make to dawn. The light which puts out our eyes is darkness to us. Only that day dawns to which we are awake. There is more day to dawn. The sun is but a morning star.

Glossary

Cyber-feminism—A virtual community that expresses a radical transgression of ordinary cultural categories in order to achieve a new social model of a feminist politics by use of the technologies of the Web and the Internet. Kenway and Langmead as well as Gur-Zeev offer analyses of this contemporary political-technological movement.

Fundamentalism—A very general and popular term. Here, Castells uses it to try to make sense of social movements. These movements develop in reaction to the disorientation of identity and loss of anchors of meaning because of the new informational economy. Fundamentalism points to the restoration of strong beliefs based on primary identities,

such as land or religion, that form new communities. They draw cultural strength and stability by having almost unbreakable, "fundamental" cultural codes of meaning.

New Age—Another popular term, with cultural dissent about its meaning. On the whole, it refers to new cultural commitments, as we indicated in Hanegraaf's treatment. By talking about an "age," the intention is to signify a very major shift in the culture, generally, away from materialism and rationality toward spirituality.

Revitalization—Wallace defined it centrally as visions or a new way of life. Revitalization movement are social movements that reconfigure the culture and try to reorganize people's everyday meanings and routines in a way that restores cultural confidence and individual motivation. A stressed and dying culture is brought back to life by a newly imagined possibility. Culture and character get new energy, new vitality.

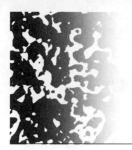

References and Resources

Abrams, M.H. 1971. *Natural Supernaturalism: Tradition and Revolution in Romantic Literature.* New York. W.W. Norton.

Althusser. L. 1971. "Ideology and Ideological State Apparatuses," in idem, *Lenin, Philosophy and Other Essays.* New York. Monthly Review Press.

Anyon, J. 1979. "Ideology and United States History Textbooks," *Harvard Educational Review* vol. 49, no. 3, August, pp. 361–385.

Apple, M. 1971. "The Hidden Curriculum and the Nature of Conflict," *Interchange* vol. 2, no. 4, pp. 27–40.

Apple, M. 1979. *Ideology and Curriculum.* Boston and London. Routledge and Kegan Paul.

Apple, M. 1982a. *Education and Power.* Boston and London. Routledge and Kegan Paul.

Apple, M., ed., 1982b. *Cultural and Economic Reproduction in Education.* Boson and London. Routledge and Kegan Paul.

Apple, M., and L. Weiss, eds., 1983. *Ideology and Practice in Schooling.* Philadelphia. Temple University Press.

Arnot, M., and J.A. Dillabough. 2000. *International Perspectives on Gender, Education and Citizenship.* London and New York. Routledge.

Bellah, R., ed. 1973. *Emile Durkheim on Morality and Society.* Chicago. University of Chicago Press.

Bernstein, B. 1973. "On the Classification and Framing of Educational Knowledge," pp. 363–393, in Richard Brown, ed., *Knowledge, Education and Cultural Change: Papers in the Sociology of Education.* London. Tavistock.

Bernstein, B. 1975. *Class, Codes and Control: Towards a Theory of Educational Transmissions.* London. Routledge and Kegan Paul.

Bernstein, B. 1996. *Pedagogy, Symbolic Control and Identity.* London. Taylor and Francis.

Black, M., ed., 1961. *The Social Theories of Talcott Parsons: A Critical Examination.* Englewood Cliffs, NJ. Prentice-Hall.

Bottomore, T., and M. Rubel, eds., 1956. *Karl Marx: Selected Writings in Sociology and Social Philosophy.* Harmondsworth. Penguin.

Bourdieu, P. 1973. "Cultural Reproduction and Social Reproduction," pp. 71–112, in R. Brown, ed., *Knowledge, Education and Cultural Change.* London. Tavistock.

Bourdieu, P. 1990. *In Other Words: Essays towards a Reflexive Sociology.* Stanford. Stanford University Press.

Bourdieu. P., and J.C. Passeron. 1977. *Reproduction: In Education, Society and Culture.* London. Sage.

Bowles, S., and H. Gintis. 1976. *Schooling in Capitalist America.* New York. Basic.

Brown, R., ed., 1973. *Knowledge, Education and Cultural Change.* London. Tavistock.

Buber, M. 1965. *Between Man and Man.* New York. Collier Books.

Callahan, R.E. 1962. *Education and the Cult of Efficiency.* Chicago. University of Chicago Press.

Carrette, J., and R. King. 2005. *Selling Spirituality: The Silent Takeover of Religion.* London. Routledge.

Carspecken, Phil Francis. 1996. *Critical Ethnography in Educational Research; A Theoretical and Practical Guide.* New York and London: Routledge.

Cassirer, Ernst. 1951. *The Philosophy of the Enlightenment.* Fritz Koelin and James P. Pettegrove, trs. Boston. Beacon Press.

Castells, M. 1996. *The Rise of the Network Society.* Oxford. Blackwell.

Castells, M. 1997. *The Power of Identity,* vol. 2. Oxford. Blackwell.

Collins, R. 1994. *Four Sociological Traditions.* New York and Oxford. Oxford University Press.

Collins, R. 2004. *Interaction Ritual Chains.* Princeton. Princeton University Press.

Csordas, T.J. 1994. *The Sacred Self: A Cultural Phenomenology of Charismatic Healing.* Berkeley. University of California Press.

Davis, K. and Moore, W. E. 1945. "Some Principles of Stratification," *American Sociological Review*, vol. 10, no. 2, April, 242–9.

Devereux, C. 1961. "Parsons' Sociological Theory," pp. 1–64, in M. Black, ed., *The Social Theories of Talcott Parsons*. Englewood Cliffs, NJ. Prentice-Hall.

Dreeben, R. 1968. *On What Is Learned in School*. Reading, MA. Addison-Wesley.

Durkheim, E. 1951. *Suicide: A Study in Sociology*. New York. Free Press.

Durkheim, E. 1964a. *The Division of Labor in Society*. New York. Free Press.

Durkheim, E. 1964b. *The Rules of Sociological Method*. New York. Free Press.

Durkheim, E. 1973. *On Morality and Society*, R. Bellah, ed. Chicago. University of Chicago Press.

Durkheim, E. 1995. *The Elementary Forms of Religious Life*, K. Fields, tr. New York. Free Press.

Emerson. R.W. 1950. *The Complete Essays and Other Writings of Ralph Waldo Emerson*. New York. Random House.

Ergas, Oren. 2008. Yoga Philosophy of Knowledge and School Curriculum; Ph.D. dissertation. Jerusalem. Hebrew University.

Foley, Douglas A., Bradley A. Levinson and Janise Hurtig. "Anthropology Goes inside: The New Educational Ethnography of Ethnicity and Gender," *Review of Research in Education*, Vol. 25, (2000–2001), pp. 37–98.

Gamoran, A., W. Secada, and C. Marrett. 2000. "The Organizational Context of Teaching and Learning: Changing Theoretical Perspectives," in M. Hallinan, ed., *Handbook of the Sociology of Education*. New York. Kluwer Academic/Plenum.

Gane, N. 2005. *Max Weber and Postmodern Theory: Rationalization versus Re-enchantment*. New York. Palgrave.

Gay, Peter. 1969. *The Enlightenment: An Interpretation. Volume II: The Science of Freedom*. New York. Alfred A. Knopf.

Gerth, Hans, and C. Wright Mills, eds., 1946. *From Max Weber: Essays in Sociology*. New York. Oxford University Press.

Goffman, E. 1967. *Interaction Ritual: Essays on Face-to-Face Behavior*. New York. Pantheon.

Gouldner, A. 1970. *The Coming Crisis in Western Sociology*. New York. Basic.

Gramsci, A. *Selections from the Prison Notebooks*. New York. International.

Gur-Zeev, I., ed., 2003. *Critical Theory and Critical Pedagogy Today*. Haifa, Israel. Haifa University Press.

Gur-Zeev, I. 2007. *Beyond the Modern-Postmodern Struggle in Education*. Rotterdam and Taipei. Sense Publishers.

Hallinan, M. 2000. *Handbook of the Sociology of Education*. New York. Kluwer Academic/Plenum.

Hanegraaf, W. 1998. *New Age Religion and Western Culture.* Albany, NY. SUNY Press.

Hawthorn, Geoffrey, 1976. *Enlightenment and Despair: A History of Sociology.* Cambridge and New York. Cambridge University Press.

Heelas, P. 1996. *The New Age Movement.* Oxford. Blackwell.

Heelas, P., and L. Woodhead, 2005. *The Spiritual Revolution.* Oxford. Blackwell.

Held, D. 1980. *Introduction to Critical Theory.* Berkeley. University of Californian.

Horkheimer, M. 1972a. *Critical Theory.* New York. Herder and Herder.

Horkheimer, M., and T. Adorno. 1972b. *The Dialectic of Enlightenment.* New York. Herder and Herder.

Hunter, I. 1994. *Rethinking the School: Subjectivity, Bureaucracy, Criticism.* New York. St. Martin's Press.

Jameson, F. 1972. *The Prison-House of Language: A Critical Account of Structuralism and Russian Formalism.* Princeton. Princeton University Press.

Katz, M. 1968. *The Irony of Early School Reform.* Cambridge, MA, Harvard University.

Katz, M. 1971. *Class, Bureaucracy and Schools: The Illusion of Educational Change in America.* New York. Praeger.

Kenway, J., and D. Langmead. 2000. "Cyber-feminism and Citizenship; Challenging the Political Imaginary," pp. 513–540, in Arnot and Dillabough, eds., *International Perspectives in Gender, Citizenship and Education.* London and New York. Routledge.

Kincheloe, J.L. 2004. *Critical Pedagogy Primer.* New York. Peter Lang.

Lave, J. and McDermott, R. 2002. "Estranged Labor." *Outlines* vol. 4, no. 1, pp. 19–48.

Lemert, C. 1995. *Sociology after the Crisis.* Boulder, CO. Westview.

Levy, M.J. 1952. *The Structure of Society.* Princeton. Princeton University.

Lomsky-Feder, E. 2004. "The Memorial Ceremony in Israeli Schools: Between the State and Civil Society," *British Journal of Sociology of Education,* vol. 24, no. 3, July, pp. 291–305.

Luckmann, T. 1967. *The Invisible Religion.* New York. MacMillan.

Mannheim, K. 1936. *Ideology and Utopia: An Introduction to the Sociology of Knowledge.* New York. Harcourt Brace and World.

Marx, K. 1956. *Selected Writings in Sociology and Social Philosophy,* T.B. Bottomore, tr. New York. McGraw Hill.

Marx, K., and F. Engels. 1959. *Basic Writings on Politics and Philosophy.* Garden City, NY. Doubleday.

McCarthy, G.E. 2003. *Classical Horizons: The Origins of Sociology in Ancient Greece.* Albany, NY. SUNY Press.

McLaren, P., and Kincheloe J., eds., 2007. *Critical Pedagogy: Where Are We Now?* New York. Peter Lang.

McLellan, D. 1973. *Karl Marx: His Life and Thought.* New York. Harper and Row.

McLennan, G. 2000. "Maintaining Marx," pp. 43–54, in G. Ritzer and B. Smart, eds., *Handbook of Social Theory.* London. Sage.

Melucci, A. 1994. "A Strange Kind of Newness: What's 'New' in New Social Movements?" pp. 101–133, in E. Larana, H. Johnston, and J.R. Gusfield, eds., *New Social Movements: From Ideology to Identity.* Philadelphia. Temple University Press.

Melucci, A. 1996a. *Challenging Codes: Collective Action in the Information Age.* Cambridge, UK. Cambridge University Press.

Melucci, A. 1996b. *The Playing Self: Person and Meaning in the Planetary Society.* Cambridge and New York. Cambridge University.

Miller, John P., Selia Karsten, Diana Denton, Deborah Orr, and Isabella Colalillo Kates, eds., 2005. *Holistic Learning and Spirituality in Education.* Albany, NY. SUNY Press.

Mills, C.W. 1959. *The Sociological Imagination.* New York. Basic Books.

Mitzman, Arthur. 1969. *The Iron Cage: An Historical Interpretation of Max Weber.* New York. Grosset and Dunlap.

Needleman, B. 2000. "The Continuing Relevance of Georg Simmel: Staking Out Anew the Field of Sociology," pp. 66–79, in G. Ritzer and B. Smart, eds., *Handbook of Social Theory.* London. Sage.

Nisbet, R. 1965. *Emile Durkheim.* Englewood Cliffs, NJ. Prentice-Hall.

Ollman, B. 1971. *Alienation: Marx's Conceptions of Man in Capitalist Society.* Cambridge. Cambridge University.

O'Sullivan, E. 1999. *Transformative Learning: Educational Visions for the 21st Century.* Toronto. Zed Books.

Outram, Dorinda. 2005. *The Enlightenment.* Cambridge and New York. Cambridge University Press.

Parsons, T. 1951. *The Social System.* Glencoe, IL. Free Press.

Parsons, T. 1966. *Societies: Evolutionary and Comparative Perspectives.* Englewood Cliffs, NJ, Prentice Hall.

Parsons, T. 1968. "The School Class as a Social System: Some of Its functions in American Society," *Harvard Educational Review,* vol. 29, no. 4, pp. 292–318.

Ritzer, G., and B. Smart, eds., 2000. *Handbook of Social Theory.* London. Sage.

Sadovnik, Alan R. *Knowledge and Pedagogy: The Sociology of Basil Bernstein,* Wesport: Greenwood Publishing Group, 1995.

Sharp, R. 1980. *Knowledge, Ideology and the Politics of Schooling: Towards a Marxist Analysis of Education.* Boston. Routledge and Kegan Paul.

Sloan, D. 2005. "Education and the Modern Assault on Being Huan: Nurturing Body, Soul and Spirit." pp. 27–47, in John P. Miller, Selia Karsten, Diana Denton, Deborah Orr, and Isabella Colalillo Kates, eds., *Holistic Learning and Spirituality in Education.* Albany, NY. SUNY Press.

Smith, R., and P. Wexler, eds., 1995. *After Postmodernism: Education, Political and Identity.* London. Falmer.

Spring, J. 1972. *Education and the Rise of the Corporate State.* Boston. Beacon.

Strenski, Ivan. 1997. *Durkheim and the Jews of France.* Chicago and London. University of Chicago Press.

Thoreau, H.D. 1960. *Walden and* On the Duty of Civil Disobedience. New York. New American Library.

Toulmin, Stephen. 1990. *Cosmopolis: The Hidden Agenda of Modernity.* Chicago. University of Chicago Press.

Turner, Jonathan, H. 1991. *The Structure of Sociological Theory.* Belmont, CA. Wadsworth Publishing.

Vidich, A., and S. Lyman. 1985. *American Sociology.* New Haven. Yale University Press.

Wallace, A.F.C. 1956. "Revitalization Movements," *American Anthropologist* vol. 58, no. 2, April, pp. 264–281.

Weber, M. 1946. *Essays in Sociology,* in H. Gerth and C. Wright Mills, eds., New York. Oxford University Press.

Weber, M. 1947. *The Theory of Social and Economic Organization.* New York. Oxford University Press.

Weber, M. 1958. *The Protestant Ethic and the Spirit of Capitalism.* New York. Charles Scribner's Sons.

Weber, M. 1963. *The Sociology of Religion.* Boston. Beacon Press.

Weber, M. 1978. *Economy and Society,* vols. 1 and 2. Berkeley, CA. University of California Press.

Wexler, P. 1983/1990. *Critical Social Psychology.* New York. Peter Lang.

Wexler, P. 1992. *Becoming Somebody: Toward a Social Psychology of School.* London. Falmer Press.

Wexler, P. 1996. *Holy Sparks: Social Theory, Education and Religion.* New York. St. Martin's Press.

Wexler, P. 2000. *Mystical Society.* Boulder, CO. Westview.

Wexler, P. 2007a. *Symbolic Movement: Critique and Spirituality in Sociology of Education.* Rotterdam/Taipei. Sense Publishers.

Wexler, P. 2007b. *Mystical Interactions: Sociology, Jewish Mysticism and Education.* Los Angeles. Cherub Press.

Wexler, P. 2007c. "Religion as Socio-educational Critique: A Weberian Example," pp. 43–57, in Peter McLaren and Joe L. Kincheloe, eds., *Critical Pedagogy*. New York. Peter Lang.

Wexler, P., and R. Smith, eds., 1995. *After Postmodernism: Education, Politics and Identity*. London. Falmer Press.

Whimster, S. 2000. "Max Weber: Work and Interpretation," pp. 54–66, in G. Ritzer and B. Smart, eds., *Handbook of Social Theory*. London. Sage.

Whitty, G., and M. Young, eds., 1976. *Explorations in the Politics of School Knowledge*. Driffield, UK. Nafferton Books.

Willis, P. 1977. *Learning to Labour*. Westmead, UK. Saxon House.

Willis, P. 2000. *The Ethnographic Imagination*. Cambridge. Polity.

Wrong, D. 1961. "The Oversocialized Conception of Man in Modern Sociology." *American Sociological Review* vol. 26. pp. 183–193.

Wuthnow, R. 1998. *After Heaven: Spirituality in America Since the 1950s*. Berkeley, CA. University of California Press.

Index

Peter Lang PRIMERS

in Education

Peter Lang Primers are designed to provide a brief and concise introduction or supplement to specific topics in education. Although sophisticated in content, these primers are written in an accessible style, making them perfect for undergraduate and graduate classroom use. Each volume includes a glossary of key terms and a References and Resources section.

Other published and forthcoming volumes cover such topics as:

- Standards
- Popular Culture
- Critical Pedagogy
- Literacy
- Higher Education
- John Dewey
- Feminist Theory and Education

- Studying Urban Youth Culture
- Multiculturalism through Postformalism
- Creative Problem Solving
- Teaching the Holocaust
- Piaget and Education
- Deleuze and Education
- Foucault and Education

Look for more Peter Lang Primers to be published soon. To order other volumes, please contact our Customer Service Department:

       800-770-LANG (within the US)
       212-647-7706 (outside the US)
       212-647-7707 (fax)

To find out more about this and other Peter Lang book series, or to browse a full list of education titles, please visit our website:

       www.peterlang.com